Dear Dad, It's Me!

MARKEIDA L. JOHNSON

Copyright © 2016 by Markeida L. Johnson

Dear Dad, It's Me!
by Markeida L. Johnson

Printed in the United States of America.

Edited by Xulon Press.

ISBN 9781498467117

All rights reserved solely by the author. The author guarantees all contents are original and do not infringe upon the legal rights of any other person or work. No part of this book may be reproduced in any form without the permission of the author. The views expressed in this book are not necessarily those of the publisher.

Unless otherwise indicated, Scripture quotations taken from the King James Version (KJV) – *public domain.*

www.xulonpress.com

Sunni,
May your future shine as BRIGHT as your name. No longer walk in a desolate place in life. This is your time to be healed and set free!

Sincerely,
Markeeda Johnson

11-30-20

To my little sister, Melissa Ann Jones
—your short-lived life inspires me to never give up.

Rest in Peace

8/15/1975-2/18/1989

TABLE OF CONTENTS

Forewords ix
Acknowledgments xiii

Part One: Dear Daddy
1 My First Love 23
2 The Reflection 26
3 The Hot Summer Day 30
4 The Orange Soda 32
5 The Yellow Cadillac 34
6 The Big Move 37
7 The Marriage 41
8 The Father Challenge 46
9 The Touch 49
10 The Teenage Years 52
11 The Car Wreck 58
12 Sweet Sixteen 67
13 The Reveal 70
14 The Phone Call 74
15 The Trip 78
16 The Birth 81
17 The Party 86
18 Real Love 91
19 The Release 97

Part Two: Dear God

20 Why Me 103
21 The Rescue. 107
22 The Broken Cycle 111
23 The Trust Issue. 115
24 The Father (God) 119
25 The Perfect Life 124

Part Three: Dear Husband

26 I'm the Father. 133
27 The Walls 137
28 The Love 142
29 The Validation 147

Part Four: The Closure

30 The Reconciliation. 153
31 The Visit. 159
32 The Epiphany 163
33 Let It Go. 166

Foreword 1

I met Markeida in 1994 at age nineteen when she was a broken-hearted young lady. She was a single mother who was trying to give her son a life she always wanted. She had major issues with her father for not being there for her. Markeida was on a long hard journey to find out who she was and how she could contribute to those who suffered the same type of life she was experiencing.

Now that I've been married to her for twenty-one years, I have seen her grow tremendously. She has matured from that little girl looking for acceptance and purpose to a woman that is goal-driven to fulfill God's assignment for her life. She is a Minister of God who is attending college to obtain a degree in psychology. Her dream has always been to be an advocate for the lost youth, and with dedication she will open up a non-profit organization to build up the fatherless generations.

Markeida Johnson, in my opinion, is the poster child for overcoming the fatherless obstacle. She is becoming someone that can and will make an impact on this world.

Loving husband,

Gary A. Johnson

Foreword 2

Markeida began to write about herself and her dad as a tool to help deal with the empty place in her heart. She never felt she fit in with her peers being a PK (preacher's kid), going through adolescents without her dad, losing her younger sister at age fourteen, and moving from place to place while her mother Evangelized. When she revealed that her memoirs were going to be turned into a book, I agreed she should share her story to help other fatherless young people. I believe her experiences can help others overcome their pain, their struggle, and their fight to find identity (in self and God) as she has done.

As I've watched Markeida grow up from the age of ten, I witnessed she was never able to see the talented, beautiful, and intelligent person she is and always was. I once told her she was going through these hardships to help others with like passions. I've seen her become stronger and wiser because of the things God allowed her to overcome. I now see her as being free and no longer stuck in the past. Lives have already begun to change because of her testimony and because she has stepped in her purpose, when others read her book the words will come alive in them.

Truly she has plenty to tell from all her life's experiences. I believe this is just the beginning of a great ministry coming through her.

Yours Truly,
Bishop D. Gipson

Acknowledgments

To my mother, Bishop Ann T. Baker, thank you for all the times I didn't understand your choices but you showed me that true dedication to God is the ultimate choice. It was your love and prayers that propelled me forward. I love you immensely.

To the love of my life, Elder Gary A. Johnson—This book would be much harder to obtain if it were not for your encouragements and belief in me. You are one of the reasons I have survived. Thank you for being an extension of God's love and affection. I love you better after twenty-one years of marriage. ("two shall be one flesh" Eph. 5:31 KJV)

To my adult babies, Daryus, Zaccheus, and Cornelius— Thank you for knowing my story and never judging me, but instead encouraging me to go forth in writing my testimony.

My life would be incomplete if you were not in it. I love each of you tremendously.

To my brother, Michael M. Crawford—We share the same story and this is our turn to transform our futures to brighter ones. Thank you for being my brother and loving me in your own special way. I love you like crazy!

To my pastor, Apostle Mandy Hamilton—Thank you for all the hours, days, months, and years you prayed me through each test and trial. You are a true warrior to be in battle for a vessel like me. You knew my entire story before I even knew there was one. I love and appreciate you unbelievably.

To my flame, Bishop Debra Gipson—Thank you for allowing me to grow in God by serving at your feet. There is no greater position in God I hold dearer than to serve you. You allow me to stay humble yet move in the calling and purpose God has for me. I love you always.

To my Powerhouse Family—What would I be without my brothers and sisters in Christ? The Blood of Jesus has made us inseparable. I love each of you and thank you for

Acknowledgments

your excitement and encouragement to go forth in the calling God has for me.

To my daddy, Marcus L. Jones, you are the reason for my testimony and we both acknowledge and receive that fact with open arms and gratitude. God is doing a great work in us and I'm glad you are now a part of the triumphant blessings being bestowed on me. I love you infinitely.

INTRODUCTION

It is so easy to play victim when we feel like we've been wronged. To always see how you are mistreated and overlooked are sure signs that the victim card is pulled out on many occasions. In every situation you seem to find yourself in the "woe is me" outlook. How pitiful must it be to be around someone who can't seem to find the silver lining in the situations that simply come to make them stronger? Who wants to be around anyone that always has a sad story or dreary outlook on life? No one. No matter how good life is, there seems to be a dark cloud hanging over their head. Well, that was me—I was a pessimistic person with no highlight in my days, always feeling sorry for myself. To move from victim to victor was a challenge I had to overcome to move past my emotional scars. I'd grown tired of feeling depressed over the smallest upsets. The energy I wasting everyday on sulking from my past hurts and pain was overwhelming. There were times I struggled to simply get out of bed for my family. It seemed like a battle for life to move forward.

My first order of business to move from that negative space was focusing on what I spoke. Proverbs 18:21 states that death and life are in the power of the tongue; and they that love it shall eat the fruit thereof. It took me years to truly understand that I was receiving that which I was speaking. I was constantly speaking "I am not happy," "I am not beautiful," and "I don't feel loved". Yes, I was giving power to those negative feelings that kept me bound.

I did not want to face the fact that I was no longer that frightened little girl who inwardly hid herself for protection from those I felt were hurting me. I finally realized I was my biggest enemy. I just seemed to be stuck in a rut of despair—wanting to always be the victim as a fatherless daughter.

Once I began to gain control over my words, I could see my world changing. It seemed a super weight began to lift off of me, a weight that was thirty-two years old. I began to go through a process of mental cleansing merely by changing the words I was speaking to myself and about myself. I gained a more positive outlook on life, in spite of some circumstances never changing. Nevertheless, I was ready to be happy with myself, my family, and my God.

Introduction

I began to keep yearly journals of my past and present life experiences; I had no idea God was using it as a healing tool. Whenever I wanted to speak negative words, I would write it down instead. At first, I had no knowledge that my negative words lost their power when I wrote them rather than speaking them out loud. Then as time went on, I began to feel less and less depressed. I was no longer eating the bitter fruit of my words.

I've learned to stop being my worst enemy. There is already plenty of negative in the atmosphere; I don't have to add to it when God has given me the authority to speak whatever I want to obtain and need. As I practiced speaking positively, I then had to begin to believe in my words. James 2:26 states, "faith without works is dead." It didn't do me any good if I didn't put action to what I was speaking. I had to believe that I could be whole, or that I could be happy, or that I do feel beautiful, without validation from anyone. I had to put these words into action before I could be loosened from these strongholds.

Do I feel strong every single day? Of course not, but the difference now is that I don't allow myself to fall into a deep, depressive slumps of despair. I look at myself in the mirror and see the flaws, and yet I still brush my teeth, comb my hair, put on the best outfit for the day, and walk out of my house with the confidence that I'm a changed woman.

As you go further into this book, you will find it is divided into three sections of "dads": My dad—my earthly dad; God—my heavenly dad; and my husband—dad to our boys; and then the closure. You will follow my journey as I traveled to reach the full potential God had for me because of being a fatherless daughter. I have allowed myself to be transparent through my circumstances and decisions so that others can see that no matter what life dishes out to you, anyone can overcome obstacles if they desire. There are some real truths that will make me vulnerable to judgments and ridicule by those who may not understand the effect of pain and rejection when making life decisions. I make no apology for where I was in those crucial times in my life, and offer no apology for where I am now. God has shown a tremendous amount of grace and mercy towards me, and I am appreciative of where He has brought me from and absolutely excited about where He is taking me. I am no longer a victim of my circumstances but one who has overcame by the words of my testimony. I know that as long as I allow God to continue to lead me down the path He would have me go, I can't go wrong.

Thank you for choosing to read my book, and I pray that you are blessed by my life's testimony.

Part One
DEAR DADDY

Chapter 1
MY FIRST LOVE

When I think of the word *daddy*, it is a term of endearment. It brings a warm feeling to the heart; a feeling of security, love, and faith. The first time I remember feeling love was for you. You were the man who showed me what it was to feel the sensation of being someone's sweetheart. There was nothing corrupt about my feelings for you because you were my daddy, my hero, my protector, my provider. When I looked at you, there was no wrong in my eyes. You were the purest form of a man I thought I would ever know. You were tall, dark, and handsome. You carried yourself with dignity and prestige. You were admired by many. You were a hard worker, always wanting more, always wanting better. I believed in who you were. I believed that you would always be there for me. I never thought for one moment that things would end, that the bond we had as daddy and daughter would someday break. Besides, you were my hero. You were rescuing me from an unknown life of hardship. You were my superman. There was nothing you could do to disappoint me, and even if you did, my love for you was so strong, it blinded me from seeing any wrong you could've been doing

Along the way of life, things began to change. I no longer held that same esteem for you. There are many unanswered questions that I've had my entire life. Did you know you were my first love? Did you know that you were my example of love? Did you know the impact your love would have on me for the rest of my life? Did you ever consider how important you would be in the decisions I would make in trying to find my lasting love? I knew how to love you, but you didn't know how to love me back. As I grew up and began to learn what love was all about, I learned that love was about mistakes and forgiving. I knew that family was supposed to stick together no matter what obstacles were in our path. I believed you were my hero, even when things began to turn for the worst. I knew my love for you was real, in spite of the tearing and the ripping away of my heart. I could not forget that I called you Daddy. I didn't know how to turn off my love like a light switch. I only knew how to trust, and believe that the pain I was beginning to feel would someday end.

Chapter 2

THE REFLECTION

In my opinion, photos speak loud and always capture the moment. As I look back through old photos I see myself being happy, satisfied, loved, but vulnerable mainly because of my age of two. There's one picture in which you are holding me, protecting me, caring for me, giving the appearance that I'm loved. My expression in the photo shows I am not concerned about anything, no fear that you may drop me or cause harm to me. I can only imagine that I'm feeling safe and secure in your arms. The picture even reflects that maybe you are proud to be a father, proud to be holding your daughter in your arms. I don't see any imperfections or any struggles that may have been going on; it only shows you being strong and tall, and there to support and protect your family. The picture captures a perfect moment in time.

The Reflection

Now that I am a parent, I think about what kind of parent I am to my children. I consider what kind of parent I want to be. While learning how to parent, I realize I wanted my children to look back on their lives to reflect on good times and good things about their parents. I wanted their memories and pictures to reflect something joyous and uplifting for them to brag about; something wonderful they can sit around the dinner table and pass on to their children. This is something that I don't have with you. My memories are diluted with rejection, abandonment, and pain; sometimes, which are over-whelming for me to think on because I could never figure out the why.

In my opinion, no one has to teach a child to love because love is already in them because we come from a loving God. However, what can be taught is hate. Hatred is taught through words, through actions, through experiences, through living life itself. Only then do we have to teach how to love again. Love, or the lack thereof, can influence a person's life in any direction, which is the reason why good, solid parenting is so important for a child's life. Solid parenting coupled with Godly teaching can alter an innocent life down the right path.

For many years I battled silently with you on how I was emotionally mistreated—better known to me as rejection.

Despite the rejections, I kept loving and forgiving, no matter how hurt I was. That child in me wouldn't let hatred take control. There's a common quote that says "there's a thin line between love and hate", and I have walked that line. When I wanted to hate you, love would not let me. Even as I loved you, hate was forever knocking at my heart.

The battle within me was great because I was torn between the two powers. Let me ask you, did you have this battle as I did? Did you really love me, but battled with hating me? There were many days that I literally tried to hate and despise you. Yet I couldn't, no matter how hard I tried. I couldn't understand why I would love someone who obviously showed no concern for me. As a young child, I couldn't comprehend how you could just move on with your life, without regard for those you left behind, who were hurting in the trenches. Without conscience effort, most of my relationships were like that, men who said with their mouths that they loved me, but their actions were far from love. There was always an ulterior motive—to get what they wanted, and then leave me with emotional baggage of loneliness and depression. Of course, none of them had any idea that they had patterned themselves after you—never fulfilling any obligation or commitment.

In retrospect, I seemed to attract the type of men who intuitively knew my personal struggles. They saw the low self-esteem, the insecurity, and the need for me to be loved by a man. It was as though they could smell the lack of fatherhood in my life, and they knew how to prey on that need. The awful part about it was that most of them never had good intentions towards me; and the otherwise good-hearted young men simply didn't know how to handle me. They didn't know how to fight for me. Without ever uttering a word of my past to them, most seemed to understand there was an empty spot in me that I was trying to fill; and they knew they could not fulfill that need. I was left unfulfilled, vulnerable, and searching for love in all the wrong places. When a fatherless child is searching for a father's love, nothing else can fill that hole, because it is only meant for a father to place his stamp on.

Chapter 3

THE HOT SUMMER DAY

I was about five or six years old, and it was a very hot summer day. Mama decided to spray us down with the water hose in the front yard to cool us down. When we were kids, this was as good as being in a six-foot, cool swimming pool, simply because of the fun and excitement of being in the water. You returned home from a hard day's work, and sat on the porch to watch us play. With all the fun we were having, I decided I wanted you to have just as much fun. Despite your attempts to prevent me from spraying you, I took the water hose from Mama and sprayed you down with all your work clothes on. At first you seemed upset, but because of all the laughter and joy, you yielded to us and joined us in creating one of the best memories I have of you. As I think back, it seemed as though we were complete as a family. Something so simple became an iron print in my heart. At that moment I felt as though I was loved, I felt secure, I felt whole. My childlike instincts wants to ask why it had to change. Why did I have to eventually feel alone and insecure about something that God ordained? Family life was never meant to be painful; yes, there would be struggles, but you stick together and overcome every obstacle. The family experience should be there to encourage one another, to love one another, and to embrace one another. Yes, of course families have issues and problems; nevertheless, the object of commitment is to press through all the hardships.

I've searched my heart inside and out to find the good things to remember about you, but there are either too many hurtful memories, or a huge time gap where you were not present in my life. Yes this is a good memory, which soon was overshadowed by family struggles that would change my life forever. Yet, I held on to this memory because it brought my heart a smile even when I wanted to cry.

Chapter 4
THE ORANGE SODA

There was one time when you took us to church with you because you and Mama didn't go to the same church. I remember I was reluctant to go with you this time, but I was made to go anyway. I don't necessarily remember the church service itself, I just remember after church they were selling refreshments and I really wanted an Orange Crush Soda. When I asked to have one your reply was "No." It appeared all the other children had some type of snack. So I wasn't thinking that maybe you didn't have the money, or that it was just too late in the night for a young child to have this caffeinated drink; the only thing that resonated was your stern "No." Your answer just latched on to my spirit, maybe because so many things seemed to be going on when you and Mama were on the brink of splitting up. I'm sure that as a child there were many "No" answers given to me just because I was a kid; but that particular time stuck with me all these years. As that little girl, I couldn't understand why things had to be so bad. I couldn't get past the fact that the other kids walking around with the same soda or some type of snack I wanted. I couldn't understand why they were so special that they got one—and apparently I wasn't special enough. Now as I reflect on it, it wasn't the fact of not receiving the soda, as much as the feeling that came with the answer. It just felt like I was rejected and undeserving to receive what I saw everyone else receiving. Maybe I simply didn't need the soda, but my mind couldn't process that concept. I could only focus on your response to me and how I felt afterwards.

The effects of a simple situation can alter the larger pattern of one's mindset, just as this one did for me. Something so innocent and insignificant had a powerful impact on me when it came to life situations where "no" was the answer. Hearing "no" would instantly make me feel rejected. I would shut down and retreat to my inner self, to sulk about someone else's determination for my life. Ultimately, I was giving others the power over my emotions. What a miserable place to be in life.

Chapter 5
THE YELLOW CADILLAC

I believe you and Mama were still together when you bought that yellow Cadillac. I'm not positive where we were going that day but you and Mama were having a heated discussion about not letting us eat in your car. I remember crying because I couldn't figure out why you were making this into a big deal about us. Why was a car more important than us? Why couldn't you see how unhappy your children were? We just wanted you to love us like you loved everybody else and everything else you deemed important. If you did indeed love us, it was really hard to decipher, especially because of the tension between you and our mother. It just seemed we, as your family, were in the way of your progress. Whatever the reason, it has affected us in ways that have lasted for years and years. Of course, now I see the importance of keeping things, like your car and house, nice and neat. However, maybe the situation should have been handled differently; not in front of us. As a child, all I understood was we were another problem for you, and that was hard to get past.

As adults, we focus on the wrong things—things that really amount to nothing at the end of the day. We forget what's really important, like family. We forget the vows we made to love and cherish our families, and we easily stress over the small stuff. In a child's mind, even if the whole family is sleeping under a bridge, as long as they have both their mama and daddy there to comfort them, then nothing else matters. But as adults, we want everything to be perfect in front of others. We want to impress somebody else, forgetting to just be there in whatever capacity you can for your family. That's what was missing in our family; somebody was trying to "keep up with the Jones," so to speak. In the meantime, we kids were suffering, we simply wanted to be loved and cherished. In the end, the yellow Cadillac that caused me to cry should not have been so important that it would accelerate the break-up of a family. In my mind, I blamed myself for the whole disagreement, because I was the one wanting to eat the French fries in the car. Although, I know now the breakup had nothing to do with the food, just think of all the years of feeling (what if I just didn't cry over the food and made a scene), if that conversation was spoken in private. As parents, we have to be careful what we speak to one another in front of our children. A young mind is so impressionable, and it is not able to categorize adult conversations. I have used this memory in my own family to filter what I spoke to my husband when I didn't agree with what was going on. Fix the situation away from innocent ears.

Chapter 6
THE BIG MOVE

By the time I was seven years old, Mama said she had seen enough pain in our hearts and in our eyes. I'm sure that whatever she was dealing with personally was also overwhelming and contributed to making that final decision to move forward with life. We packed our possessions and moved away from friends and home as we knew it. It seemed like we had moved a million miles away from you. Although things were rough back home, nothing prepared me for not seeing you at all. I never wanted you out of my life. I never thought I wouldn't see you, or hug you, or just simply hear your voice. But that's what we got out of the deal, a permanently broken home. I remember asking when we would see you again, wondering if you wanted to see us anymore. The only thing I knew was that Daddy was missing, and a great sadness overcame me. That sadness walked with me for many years.

As a kid, wanting or needing your money never crossed my mind. I only wanted to be loved by both Daddy and Mama. I prayed to God many days that he would fix you all. I wished every night I went to bed, that when I woke up in the morning you would be there. But morning after morning, my prayers proved to not work for me. I couldn't help but wonder if it was my fault that Daddy left us. Was it because I sprayed you with the water hose when you said not to? Was it that the time I wanted an orange crush soda and cried when you said no? Was it because we wanted to eat in your new car and you didn't want us to? I thought maybe it was something I didn't even realize I had done that upset you enough to leave us. I thought *I* had done something so bad that it would cause you to walk out of our lives, and never look back.

The craziest thing about this move was we moved in with your sister. I don't know how that decision came to be, but I thought well maybe we will get to see my daddy since we are not too far from family. Although I knew she was family, I remember her explaining to me who you were to her and I became excited because I was sure this plan would work for you and mama to get back together. So I went back to praying and begging God to please allow my parents to love each other again so you could love us, the kids, again. The saddest thing throughout the months we stayed with your sister is, I never saw you. My heart was so heavy because all I wanted was my daddy. I remember standing on the porch and wishing I would see that yellow Cadillac pull up. However, day after day, no daddy!

I blamed myself for all those things I thought I had done wrong. I imagined I made you not only divorce my mother, but me too! (What a burden to carry!) I remember thinking that I could fix it if I remembered special holidays like your birthday, Father's Day, and Christmas; I figured those holidays I could make it all about you. I would always reach out to you on those occasions to show you that I loved you in spite of what was going on in our lives. Wherever we moved, I would call to let you know where we were. I wanted to be sure that if you decided to talk to us, you'd have the phone number to contact us. Your number didn't change for years, and I had committed it to memory. That way, I never had to search for it.

With my very limited resources as a child, I could not break the year-after-year pattern of not seeing you. It seemed that all my efforts were for naught; absolutely nothing changed for the better. What a horrible feeling, trying to bridge the gap between us, but making no progress. Why weren't the adults trying to fix it? I was angry because I didn't understand the process. This process of being a fatherless daughter was more than I wanted to bear. But it was a cross I had no choice but to carry.

Chapter 7

THE MARRIAGE

I was about eleven or twelve years old when I heard the crushing news that you were remarried. I moved past all the hurt, straight to pure anger for you. I hated you for a long time, yet I loved you so much. Abandonment and rejection packed their suitcases and moved into my heart. I could not figure out why you would divorce my mother with three kids and marry another woman with four kids. Worse, you continued to reject the ones you knew were hurting. You seemed to be consciously abandoning us, never to look back and check on us. What could you have been thinking, to be so cruel to innocent children; to children who loved you and only wanted your love in return?

Yes, I hated your new wife too! I don't necessarily blame her for anything, because I don't know the whole story on how you two got together, however, I felt like she knew our situation. She knew us well enough, through the church, to be a little more sympathetic to us. Maybe she didn't like my mother. I don't know what, if anything, my mother might have done to her; however, someone should have been adult enough to recognize that there would be lifelong effects for the children. I remember being in your new wife presence a few times before we moved away. I remember her kids and my siblings and I playing together. I considered her kids my friends; but here we are, in a serious crisis now. How can I accept that my friends are experiencing a life with a man I called Daddy, and I'm being alienated from his life? Their life was the one I longed for, cried for, wished for. I didn't mind sharing you, my daddy—I just wanted to be a part of the experience.

There's no logical explanation to this kind of behavior. No matter what the circumstances the adults were going through, why couldn't somebody see the children? Why did it have to be so much hurt and pain? I just didn't want to feel invisible anymore, but there was nothing I could do to stop the pain. No amount of tears, and no fervent wishing away the pain could stop the abyss of loneliness I felt on a daily basis.

Without having any accurate information on her feelings, I am plagued with wondering what amount of insecurity could a woman possesses that she could be an accessory to keeping a father from his first family in order to save her own? Many times I've thought, which may not be true, you were still in love with my mother and your new wife knew it, so she had to make sure you stayed away to avoid doubting your love for her? Nothing made sense to a young, fatherless girl; and it still doesn't to a grown woman who now has her own family. I just can't seem to find the logical thinking behind purposely allowing children to hurt. The icing on the cake was when you intentionally adopted other precious, innocent babies, and raised them as your own. Yet never reached out to your first family who needed you desperately. So this was two different sets of children receiving your love and support and my siblings and I were getting nothing. What a mental trip I went through, trying to place all these events into perspective.

I am a grown woman now, married, and with children of my own. I can view things a little differently now, when it comes to your wife's perspective. Although it seemed she was not a positive influence in how you viewed us, I don't know the midnight talks you two had regarding us. Even if she encouraged you to do more and you refused, I just wish she could have stepped up and done more to pave a way for us to have a relationship with the new family. Especially with the fact that I was relentless in reaching out to you and. To try to make sense of all this, I think, maybe she was trying to protect her castle. Maybe she was thinking she had to make a life for her children and we would be an interference. Maybe she felt like this was her way of being happy, which was to have you to herself.

To the parents reading this book, if you are in a relationship with a person who has children previous to you; don't allow the children to suffer because of your hang-ups with the other parent of the children. Don't allow the new children in your life to be rejected especially if you have children of your own going into the new relationship. It is not the children's fault of why the parents couldn't work it out. Of course, you can't control the parent raising the children in how they respond to you, but please make a valiant effort to ensure the children know the parent that left loves them. Nevertheless, the children are always caught in the crossfire of separation. I couldn't think of a reason why she would hate us too, but I questioned it countless times. I could only go on the response or lack thereof to judge my feelings on.

The Marriage

Daddy I only wanted a phone call from you, or a card in the mail, or even a short visit every now and then, to ensure I wasn't forgotten. I never dreamed of anything extravagant from you, just simply for a father to love me regardless of the situation.

Chapter 8
THE FATHER CHALLENGE

When we say that children are a responsibility, it can sound as though they are a burden. Without thought, we put them in categories like we put things that we don't have much regard for. For instance, it is responsible of me to put gas in my car; or it's responsible of me to wash my clothes, or clean my house when it's dirty. These things don't hold much value to us although they are things that must be done to function in everyday life. When we say a father should take care of his responsibility, we are in essence saying that he doesn't have to love his kids, just take care of them financially. Although money is indeed helpful when raising children, it is not enough. A father who truly loves his children, and cares for their well-being recognizes it's not a just a responsibility; it is an honor to love and take care of what he helped to create. It will no longer be a chore, but something you love doing. I challenge you fathers that feel like it's a chore to take care of your kids to change how you think; see if you find greater peace about the situation. Your children are a part of you and when you neglect your children you are rejecting yourself. In my opinion, a parent who can reject their own children could not possibly love themselves when they know they are hurting the children they vowed to love.

I've often wondered how a parent can love someone else's children over their own. How can you bring children into your house and welcome them as your own, and then turn your back on the children you created, who you know need you? I have never been able to figure that out and the pain has only increased over time, knowing that I was never good enough for you to fight for me. When I could visibly see there is a fight in you because you took on four other children, plus foster and adopted children. I cried many nights for you to fight for me, for you to show me I was worth the fight. I have no problem with those other children needing love too, but what about me?

So fathers see your children as a prize possession that deserves everything you can give them. Someone you respect and teach to grow to be mature functioning adults. They didn't ask to be here, so they shouldn't have to suffer the consequence of your actions. Many man may use the excuse I didn't have my father growing up or my father was in my life but didn't teach me how to be a man. We want to place blame somewhere else for our short comings; when in reality as adults we are in control of what we do, not what somebody else didn't do. Be the father that you wished you had. Be the father opposite to the negative way you saw growing up. All it takes is a made up mind that you will be the best father you can possibly be to your seed of this earth. Whatever effort, on the side of right, you have to do to prove you will fight for your child, DO IT!!! Your child(ren) need it from you.

Chapter 9
THE TOUCH

At the age of twelve I was molested three times by someone we called a friend of the family; he was someone I saw as a father figure. This was a person I trusted to do what was right in the eyes of God, his wife, and his child. How devastating it was to look in the eyes of this family friend I loved purely and genuinely, who was now hurting me; touching me in places that no one had a right to go. This man thought he could tread on my emotions, my search for true, acceptable love. I thought I had done something horrible to receive this type of treatment. I thought maybe I did not deserve to be happy and at peace. I thought maybe my desire for true love was a curse for me. I could not seem to find what I was looking for. No male in my life had the capacity to love a little girl like me. It seemed that *most* of the male figures I looked up to for security and acceptance let me down in huge proportions.

For many years, I blamed myself for breaking up his family, when he and his wife split up. If I had never told what he'd done, then maybe he'd still have a family. Family, the very thing I had been searching for; now I felt partly to blame for it crumbling. I felt so ashamed that his daughter was growing up without him, like I had to grow up without you. The effects of his abuse caused me to internalize every emotion of fear and mistrust for men. The "touching" took place at night, when I would have to be around him while spending the night at my god-sisters house. I was very confused about how to handle this situation. I couldn't help but think it was my own fault that this was happening to me over and over. I couldn't figure out how to stop it, because I was sure he would throw me away like you did. This was my god-sister's husband, by the way. She was someone I respected and loved dearly. Telling her that this monster, her husband, was touching me was devastating to consider, and I had to figure it out how I was going to expose this devil. However, I found the strength to tell when I thought my sister might be next. I couldn't imagine him touching her and then I stay silent; to sit back and do nothing about it was tormenting me. I could not bear to think of her feeling the way I did, battling this horrible emotion, — so I told my mother. She immediately went into action to protect us. However, again I felt I would not be loved once again. I knew I didn't want him touching me, but I also felt that I was responsible for someone else not loving me anymore. Who would protect me now? You were nowhere near for me to cry to or to ask for your protection in this situation. My super hero, my daddy, had vanished from my life while I laid vulnerable to be prey for those beast of men who did not respect the little girl in me.

For years I struggled with insecurities at night. I would wrap myself in covers to insure no creep would come in to touch me as I slept. I didn't feel safe in my own skin and thought I was not worth anything to anybody. All because of a wrong touch.

Chapter 10
THE TEENAGE YEARS

As a teenager, I went through many things, like most teens do. Even if a teen grows up in a loving, two-parent home, there are going to be certain psychological changes that will take place. There is a change to the mental state of a person when they become teenagers, through no effort or intent of their own. I think that's why most teenagers seem as though they have lost their minds—they are simply experiencing this change as part of being a teenager. Now, think of a young person without any proper guidance to direct their path on the straight and narrow. These teenagers are trying figure it out on their own, not understanding that the path they're taking could be the wrong one. A child needs the affirmation from their father to bring security to the path in life they are taking. The father represents the authority of the home. The father represents the foundation on which the family will stand. Without that proper structure, the family will not be able to stand in its full capacity. So our teens are growing up without a sure foundation on who they are and where they belong.

I had convinced myself that if I never stopped calling you or reaching out to you, that you would eventually accept me. So I continued to pursue your love. (Again, I stress, never wanting your money, your big house, or your fancy car; only wanting you). So that relentless drive bled over into my relationships with men. I thought I had to go through hoops to get men (not boys) to love me. And of course in the end I came up empty handed, feeling unloved, lonely, and vulnerable.

Words cannot explain the many nights I cried because you were not there for me. As a young lady growing up, a father plays a major role in her development. Socially, physically, and mentally a true father should be there to develop those stages of growth. People may feel like a mother is the only one the girl needs when she hits that puberty stage, because we only think of the breast forming, the menstrual stage, and the changing of the body. However, a father is needed to help guide her through all those stages as well as to help keep her grounded. Boys appear from the four corners of the earth during this process. Without a strong father's word to affirm her, most likely whatever the boy says, she believes it. Just as a male goes through developmental stages a young girl does as well. I never got that talk from a male point of view. Daddy, you never told me I was beautiful, so when dude around the way told me I was, I paid attention. Daddy, you never told me I was smart and strong, so when that perverted adult male told me those words it opened me up to think he had my best interest in heart—only to later find out he saw my search for a daddy and played on those emotions. I was so exhausted in my teen years from searching and looking for that right affirmation. I ran into so many dangerous road blocks because I thought the person standing before me was the one who could give me what I was looking for; when in the end their intentions were all wrong.

Love is a powerful thing, and not being loved can be just as powerful. People can live destructive lives searching for the love that they feel is lacking. When you lack love in your life it's hard to give or receive love. That's why we need Jesus to show us the way. John 3:16 states, "For God so loved the world, that He gave is only begotten son, that whosoever believeth in him should not perish but have everlasting life."

The Teenage Years

Jesus was God's prize possession, which He gave to this world to show us how to love unconditionally. Jesus took on the sins of this world that we may be saved; and He showed the world how we ought to love one another. Real love is a hard thing to acquire. Love is a word that is loosely used; it is spoken regularly, but rarely genuinely displayed.

When I was fourteen, we lived a couple of houses down from an abandoned house. One summer day, I was walking in our neighborhood just to get out of my family's house. I wasn't going far, just from our house to the main road and back again. I had actually planned on walking that several times back and forth just to think things through. On my way back from the main road, I noticed there were three older teenage boys standing in front of the abandoned house. I had never seen these boys in our neighborhood before, but I wasn't nervous. We lived in an area where people were always walking, so I didn't think there was anything strange about it. However, as I approached the house, two of the boys walked up to me and grabbed me. They took me in the abandoned house and tried to take advantage of me. One covered my mouth, while the second one held my hands, and the third one was at my feet. I tried to scream, tried to fight them off, but they were too powerful for me. I remember laying there crying and calling on Jesus in my mind. The guy at my feet ripped my panties off, but then he suddenly stopped. They were talking, but every word sounded muffled because fear had gripped me. Within a few moments, all three let go of me and ran out of the house. I lay there for a moment, trying to get myself together and to decipher what just happened. I know God protected me from further trauma. However, although there was no physical trauma, this incident took me on a roller coaster of emotional ups and downs.

After this situation, I couldn't help but wonder if I was meant to carry some burden through life, a burden I was too young to bear. My self-esteem was challenged to the point where I could not see any worth for myself in this life. I began to even question if God loved me. My home was so broken to the point that my siblings and I were separated from each other for a span of time. My sister and I moved in with other people, while my brother lived somewhere else. I felt lost and misplaced in this world. I couldn't figure out what good this life had to offer me. I questioned God, "Why was I born? What was the purpose of this hard life?" God never gave me an answer although I questioned many times. I contemplated ending my life since I just couldn't find any real meaning to it anyway. It wasn't until many years later that I could see all the trials and tribulations working together for my good.

I don't know specifically what spooked those boys away, but I chose to believe that the love Jesus had for me caused them to leave me untouched. I had to deal with the emotional distress from the experience, but remained physically unharmed. In that situation God showed me He loved me enough to protect me and for that I am grateful.

Chapter 11
THE CAR WRECK

On January 28, 1989, my sister, my mother, four other adults, and I loaded into a canary-yellow hatchback Volvo and we headed to Tyler, Texas for a church service. On this infamous day, which is also my brother birthday, we were in a car accident. My sister was only thirteen, and I was fourteen. We had just stopped at the gas station to fill up and get snacks for the trip. The trip was only about two and one half hours from home, so we would not have to be uncomfortable long. Once our carload was on the highway, my sister and I decided to take a nap because we knew it would be a long night. First there was the church service, and then we would be driving right back home the same night.

As we were traveling on Hwy I20, between Minden, LA and Shreveport, LA the tire on the car blew out, causing the

The Car Wreck

car to spin out of control on a bridge. I remember hearing a loud sound, and within seconds the car was banging against the sides of the bridge. The force of the spin kept me from moving, and all I could do was look out the window as the car became airborne, spinning uncontrollably. My first instinct was to grab my sister, who was sitting right next to me, but I could not get a good grip on her. As I tried to turn to get a better hold, I felt a pressure on my chest, holding me down. I struggled to move, but could not hold my sister. It seemed like forever before the car came to a stop. As the car stopped and everyone inside began to assess themselves, my first thought was my sister. Horrifyingly, she was no longer sitting next to me. I tried to tell the others in the car that my sister was no longer there, but I think everyone was in shock from the accident, and didn't realize the implications of what I was saying. Yet, simultaneously, everyone understood my words, and began to rush out of the car. One other person had been injured, but everyone else who was uninjured, jumped out of the car in search for my sister. We began to frantically look for her on the freeway and on the sides of the bridge, which also had an underpass. The passing moments seemed like forever when we could not find her.

We finally found her—my sister, your daughter. She had been thrown from the car and was now pinned underneath it. She was severely injured with burns and abrasions from being dragged by the spinning car. I wanted to panic and lose my mind the very moment I saw her hair underneath the driver side tire, but I held it together. Instantly, everything I'd learned in health class only a few days earlier came back to me. We had talked about what to do with a person with head injuries; and after finding my sister under the car, it was clear she had injuries. With blood coming from her head, I felt frantic for her life. I tried to climb under the car to see if she was conscience. At first glance, I wasn't sure if she was dead or alive; I tried talking to her to see if she could respond to me. Thankfully, within minutes she began with moans and groans. I frantically called out her name so she would recognize that it was me. As this was going on, my mother and pastor tried to lift the car off of her. Even with all the adrenaline and desire to move the car they could not. We later found out that it was for the best, since the effects of suddenly moving the car could have sent her into shock.

After a few moments of trying to stimulate her, she began to call out for help, for someone to please help her. She would call on Jesus, and then she would call out for our mother.

All the while, I was there, speaking to her, asking her questions that she should have been able to answer. I was trying to evaluate whether she was suffering from a serious head injury. With every question, I dreaded to hear the answers. However, I was determined to never leave her side. By the grace of God, she knew the answer to every question I asked. At my young age of fourteen, I had no medical experience but I was trying my best to be there for her, and keep her from slipping away from us.

All the adults were working hard to see to her and the other injured person. Things just seemed like pure chaos for a long while. I could not believe this was happening to my sister. She was the one person I could depend on to be there with me. She was my shadow, so to speak. We were one another's strength. We were experiencing all this misfortune together, and I could not imagine living without her. This was definitely too much to handle.

Out of all the commotion, the one thing that stuck in my mind was that she called on the two people who were most important to her; the ones on whom she could depend, no matter what. She called earnestly for God and Mama! As she lay on that hard pavement with that hot and heavy car stretched across her body, she knew who to call on for her strength. It seemed as though time stopped as I lay on the ground with her, holding her hand, trying to give whatever consolation to her the pain and agony she was experiencing. I wished over and over again in my mind that I could trade places with her. Nothing inside of me wanted to live through this crisis, and all the while I also thought that she was not going to make it herself. I remember feeling so helpless, as I had felt so many times before. I was in a situation where I had no control over what was happening to us. I was wishing this was just a bad dream and that I would eventually wake up. The problem was though, that once again this was reality. I was not imagining this neither was I dreaming this, but it was really happening. We were facing yet another one of the many life-changing circumstances in our short lives.

I remember that an ambulance eventually came down the freeway, in route to the hospital with another patient. The driver stopped to assist us and called for rescue; at this point the car was still on top of my sister. It seemed as though only a few moments later the whole area was full of people, cars, and rescue personnel. There was now a lot of commotion and running back and forth; everything was happening so fast. I certainly felt lost in what to do or where to go. My adrenaline was pumping so high that I never noticed that I was injured and needed to go to the hospital. The only thing I could focus on was that my sister, who no was longer sitting next to me in the car. The one and only constant person in my life was hanging on to life by a thread. I couldn't imagine what I would do without her. It was too unbearable to even consider that she may not live.

Once the rescue squad lifted the car, they took my sister to a nearby hospital. Eventually, we all were whisked away in cars and ambulances to get checked out at the hospital. As we all lay in the hospital we heard the hospital codes that my sister had passed away. At first I didn't understand what the codes meant, but I distinctly remember hearing one of the nurses calling out my sister's name as she ran past my room in the ER. My heart felt as though it would fail me right then. By the grace and mercy of God they were able to resuscitate her. A few days later, they moved her to the Bossier City/ Shreveport Hospital where there were better facilities.

It was then that I reached a new level of anger for you. I felt like it took a tragedy for you to come see about her, your own daughter. In the thirteen years she lived on this earth, you couldn't see what beautiful flower she was. You turned your back on one of the most precious jewels God created. I tried loving her to make up for the love that was otherwise missing in our lives. (Of course, I wasn't perfect—I was still a sister.) I felt like I was her other mother, trying to protect her from predators and those who meant her no good. I was only fourteen so I'm not sure how well I did, but I was giving it my best effort. It wasn't until she was on her death bed that you bought things for her that now she could not use or enjoy (a two-cassette deck radio and her favorite album, *The Winans*). Those things would have been perfect for Christmas, which had just passed, or maybe her birthday, or maybe just as a "because I love" you gift. Instead, you thought it was appropriate to give her those things as she lay dying. No gift could be given to make up for the lack of a father she had in you. She suffered burns, a broken pelvic bone, broken ankle, punctured kidney, broken ribs, and major head trauma. All these things could be healed over time, but what heals a broken heart? I wondered, as she lay there for two weeks without recovering from her injuries, if she forgave you for abandoning her? I wondered if she was sad that you didn't want her to be in your life. I wondered if there was anything she needed or wanted to make right with God concerning you, before He took her home. These questions will never be answered at this point. I like to imagine that God took her because she was ready to meet Him. Maybe she didn't have anything against you. It wasn't until sometime later that I realized I was not ready to meet Him, I had too much anger in my heart for you, and I had not yet been able to forgive you or others who had hurt me. Although I wished it was me on that dying bed, God was trying to give me a chance to put it all down. All the hate and hurt I bottled up on the inside.

Doctors said she would never fully recover from her injuries. She lived two more weeks and then passed away. My sister, the only person I felt I had in my life at that time, was taken from me. The day we put her in the ground, February 25, 1989, a piece of my soul went with her. That day, I recognized how lonely my life would be without my shadow. My family had been torn apart—no father, a mother traveling and evangelizing, and my brother and I not really close—and now my only sanctuary, my sister, was gone forever. How does one recover from such a tragic life? Nothing but a true and living God can keep a person's mind from snapping during these types of life situations. Although I was not in total, perfect peace, God kept me going when I wanted to just give up. God gave me the strength to overcome the impossible. Most of all, He gave me the strength to keep loving you no matter how wounded I felt.

My mother encouraged me to love you, the man whom showed me no love. No matter how hurt I was, she would tell me that I couldn't harden my heart. She reminded me that God loves me regardless of what I do or think. Now, she could have easily allowed me to drown in those evil feelings of hatred and anger, but she told me I was better than that. I had the power to forgive and let go. And although I battled with hating you her words kept a fire burning inside me to always love you and try to establish a relationship with you, although it was never accepted by you.

Chapter 12
Sweet Sixteen

It is common knowledge that turning sixteen is supposed to be sweet. Sixteen is considered the turning point in a teenager's life, going from childhood to pre-adult. In certain states, sixteen-year-olds can legally drive a car or legally get a job. Those exciting options can make a young person feel more like an adult. Sixteen is a time when a young girl or boy should be moving away from childish ways, and embarking on the adventures of becoming a young adult.

Nothing was sweet about me when I turned sixteen, because I was so wrapped up in misery. Every single moment of that day, I waited, hoping you would call me to wish me a Happy Birthday. I never wanted you to go out of the way to buy me anything, I just wanted to hear your voice; it just seemed as though your voice would make all the difference for my day. However, I was let down once again. Although all my friends were there to help me celebrate, loneliness became my best friend. I never let any of my friends see how sad I really felt on the inside. I would smile, laugh, and mingle as though everything was okay. I couldn't dare to let anybody in my three feet of personal space. The one person I wanted there, who was you, didn't want to be so I wouldn't let anybody else in. Honestly, that made me a lonely person, because no one really knew me. I spent a lot of time guarding my heart, and not enough time feeling the love from those who were trying to give it to me. I'm sure I would have made better choices if I had been able to receive true love, because that's all I was searching for, but mainly in the wrong places and from the wrong people.

There were many things that had gone horribly wrong in my life at this point. Life's situations caused me to spiral into a deep depression. I tried to hide the depression and function like there was nothing wrong. I thought that I would always be in this place of depression, so I became comfortable. I was consumed with thinking nothing would ever change for the better in my life. It felt like boys and men were my every focal point, whether I invited them into my heart, or if they came in through force. I thought that the love I needed was supposed to come from the male gender. I had no clue how to love myself first. As a matter of fact, I didn't think I was lovable. I couldn't fathom anybody really seeing me for me and loving me for real.

From the age of sixteen, I became a little destructive with how I viewed myself. I figured if no one else loved me then why should I love myself. I began to try things out that had I gotten caught up in them would have destroyed my life. I couldn't see that God was holding back the hand of the enemy so I wouldn't get wrapped up in these things that were becoming intriguing to me.

Chapter 13

THE REVEAL

I was a seventeen year old junior in high school. There was this man in my neighborhood who was pursuing me romantically. He was not someone I was attracted to physically plus I knew he was too old for me, so I resisted in the beginning. Over time he began to woo me with nice gifts and gestures. Of course that began to wear me down with accepting him in my space. I would hide the things he did for me because he was much older than me and my mother would have a fit if she found out what was going on.

He began to speak the language I was so desperately wanting to hear. Words of encouragement and affirmation to build me up. As hard as I tried not to, he finally won my heart with his cunning ways of showing me he was on my side. He began to love me like I wanted to be loved, so I began to give back to him what he wanted. Of course I didn't have much to offer, I was a junior in high school still living with her mother. So all I had to give was my conversation and myself.

Everything is always great in the beginning. He became exciting to hide and sneak around with. I thought I was falling head over hills for a man who was 12 years older than me. I thought this was everything I had been waiting for in him. I thought I was feeling good about myself and about what was going on. But I was delusional. I wanted to only feel the good and not accept the bad that was standing in my face everyday. Our secret finally got out and people including my mother was not happy with this relationship. There were people in my school that would come up to me to warn about who he really was. And out of desperation for love I rejected what they saying to me. I became very rebellious toward my mother. Almost to the point of hating her for telling me what was right. My whole spirit changed from a wounded timid little girl to a wounded aggressive young girl. This relationship opened me up to avenues that I had never experienced before.

I began to see his aggressive side toward me when he realized he couldn't control me any longer. We would argue over the smallest things and then the arguments would turn to verbal aggression towards me. There were news reports about him being in certain situations, but I didn't want to believe them. I could see all this unfolding right before, but I was certain he loved me so I wouldn't leave him. He never went as far as to hit me, but the aggression was building up so, I know eventually it was coming.

I went back into being depressed and feeling lonely. I could see he was no good for me but I didn't have the strength to get out. I began to get sick from what I thought was stress. My body was changing its normal cycle and I was too afraid to say anything to my mother. By the way, she was the one telling me to leave him alone but I wouldn't listen. March 26, 1992, I found out I was pregnant with my son. On that day it was like a light bulb came on in my head. I could see everything so clearly and I had the strength I didn't think I could find to leave this situation before it became worse. I thought about my son and how this no good life style would affect him. So I began to remove myself from the situation. I really ran for my life because if I had tarried I may have never got out.

The thing that worried me the most was how was my mother going to handle this news that I was pregnant. It took me three months to get the nerve to tell her. I was accustomed to hurt, pain, and rejection, which was what I was expecting from her. She surprised me though; she held me tight and told me everything would be okay. She assured me that she and I would work through this together. Throughout this difficult situation, God blessed our relationship to be the best it had ever been up to that point. I not only gained a better relationship with my mother, but I found out that my mother was a great friend. We began to spend a lot more time together, especially in the kitchen. It seemed I could not get enough food to feed this growing child inside me. I'm sure my mother was hurt and disappointed in me for being pregnant at such a young age. Just as any parent has dreams and aspirations for their child, she had them for me, but she never let me see her disappointment. She was always supportive of me, with all the aches and pains I had carrying this child. When I cried, she was right there to hold me and let me know that everything would be okay. When I didn't think I could wake up and live my life, she would share her story with me, and reassure me that I would make it too. The thing she told me was, I couldn't give up on myself; no matter who didn't believe in me, I had to believe in myself. That was one of the greatest battles of my life, to believe in myself; but I had to start working on it if I was going to bring this precious baby in this world.

Chapter 14

THE PHONE CALL

You and I finally planned a time for me to come visit for the summer. We'd never been to this point before, so I was extremely excited about seeing and spending daddy/daughter time with you. I hadn't seen you in three years which was at the funeral for my sister. It was a miracle that any plans had been made at all, because those kinds of plans were few and far between. I can remember only one other time in my life that I was able to come see you, and that was maybe a year before the car wreck. So needless to say, I was nervous just preparing to come. There was one problem with our plans....I did not know I was pregnant when we made plans for me to come. Of course it was very upsetting for me to have to tell you that I was expecting a little baby. School was ending soon, so I thought I should let you

The Phone Call

know about my condition. With all the things I was going through, the thought of coming to see you brought calm to my aching heart.

I called to confirm that I was still coming for a visit and to tell you about my situation. I was hoping you would be understanding and still allow me to come. Well, of course my life was shattered by your words. You told me that your wife thought it would not be a good idea for me to come, because I may be a bad influence on her girls. You could have just put a bullet through my heart. At that moment, I couldn't take any more from you. I was ready to die. There was no more room in my heart for rejection. It was as though the breath left my body. I could feel a murderous anger in me for you that day. Not only did I not want to live, but I thought you didn't deserve to live either. What was your purpose for being alive? Was it to be a torment to me? Where you born to make sure that I could not find peace and happiness? After those thoughts flashed through my mind, I fell to the floor because my knees wouldn't hold up my weight. This was the one and only time I saw my mother break down in tears because of you. You had committed the ultimate crime of rejection, shutting me out at that low point in my life. I was already down, and you just stomped on me. It was a brutal feeling that I thought I would never recover from. I thought there was no bouncing back from this blow. I felt like you didn't stand up for me not this time or any other time in my life. The way it was conveyed to me, you allowed your wife to wear the pants in this situation. That day, I saw a greater strength in my mother raise up. She picked me up off the floor—and she didn't put me down until I could stand on my own again. Honestly, I don't know how I was able to go on from that. Nothing in me wanted to live anymore. After that call, I gave you absolute power over my mind, body, and soul. You had stripped me from every little piece of hope I held on to for reconciliation. My every thought was about you and how hurtful you made my life. Then one day I realized that I had a baby to live for. Finally, it occurred to me that I was harming my baby by being so depressed. I couldn't function in my everyday life at this point. Nevertheless, I decided to fight for myself and for my baby. I realized I could no longer conjure up hateful thoughts about you or hurtful things I could do to make you feel the same pain I was feeling. I had to figure out a way to release some of the anguish I was going through. I realized love is better than hate and began to forgive you for hurting me so deeply. I worked very hard to move past that situation by praying for us to be healed. In my opinion, you

The Phone Call

had to be dealing with something painful of your own, in order for you to hurt me to this magnitude. My way to heal was to love you all the more, no matter what. That doesn't mean I didn't cry or feel pain, but I refused to let it make me hateful towards you. I understood hating you or your wife would not fix my situation. Although hate was knocking at my heart's door, I was ready to battle for peace in me.

Chapter 15

THE TRIP

My mother and I traveled to Texas to visit a family friend when I was about five months pregnant. I had known this family since I was a small girl, so they were reliable people. While I was there, I began to feel the encouragement I needed to go on in life. We were having a good time, with great fellowship. The family friend, who was thirteen years my senior, began to give me a "father-daughter" talk, something I had never had before. I began to feel comfortable and let down my guard, the guard that kept me from trusting men. As the conversation went on, I began to trust him to not harm my emotions. I pondered over in my mind if maybe I could learn to trust in men again. Perhaps not all men were a low-life's, as I had experience them to be. Just for a short moment in time, I felt hopeful that this was real.

The Trip

Remember, nearly every man that I had respected shattered that respect in some form or fashion.

Needless to say, by the end of the conversation, he turned on me. He began to lure me into his web of lies. Things turned from the father-daughter conversation, to a sexual, ungodly one. I let that guard down, and he hooked me like a fish and reeled me in. I was confused and angry, trying to decipher what was happening. All I wanted was for someone to be there for me with no strings attached. I didn't need another sex partner, or someone claiming they loved me all for the wrong reasons. This man preyed on my vulnerability. He knew my life story, yet decided to move in for the kill. I thought I didn't deserve anything better, so I allowed him a place in my heart. He offered me support financially, emotionally, and by the end of the conversation, sexual gratification.

By this time, I was an eighteen-year-old, upcoming senior in high school who was five months pregnant. The way he offered this enticing pleasure trip was emotionally undeniable. I always knew this situation was wrong, but he offered it on a silver platter and I took the bait. It had only been two months since I was told I couldn't come to your home, so at this point I was a little angrier, and I didn't care anymore. (I continued to battle with loving you, no matter what—although I failed some days) Was I happy about making a bad decision to see a married man? NO! But I figured I wouldn't be lonely. I felt as though I was already low and couldn't feel any worse about myself, so what did I have to lose. I didn't want to be alone, and at that point, that's all that mattered to me.

As time went on, I knew deep down inside that he did not love me like he said he did. When you love someone, you don't cause that kind of pain. He knew he had shattered my trust in him, but he always had the perfect, conniving words to justify that what we were doing was okay. I stayed in this relationship for nine month, and throughout those months he was true to his word to be there for me. He was supportive in the ways he had promised, with the exception that he wasn't mine to have.

Chapter 16

THE BIRTH

On November 9, 1992 at 6:39 p.m., the Lord had mercy on me and blessed me with a healthy 7 lbs. 14oz. baby boy. He was the most beautiful baby I had ever seen. When the nurse laid him in my arms, it was the most fearful moment I had ever had. Not only was I responsible for myself, but now I had a little, innocent person to care for. I wondered what kind of parent I would be. My examples of parenting were not very strong and I couldn't help but wonder if I too would fall victim to the parenting style I had witnessed. Haunting questions briefly filled my mind. Would I abandon him? Would I not show him enough love? Or would I be too busy to see to his needs? Then I pulled my attention to this bundle of joy laying in my arms. I began to count all ten fingers and toes to make sure they were all there and perfect.

I admired his perfectly round head that was full of straight lengthy hair, as to why I had so much heart burn. As I examined my little baby, on that birthing table, I instantly knew what kind of mother I would be. I looked at the mistakes made by you and by my mother, and knew that I wouldn't make those same ones. I vowed to my baby son that I would always be there for him. I was an eighteen-year-old young single parent, but I was determined to be the best mother I could possibly be.

There was no father to admire the miracle that had grown inside me. There was no name to give him but the one you and I shared. What does that name mean to someone who's been rejected by the one man you've been named after. My whole name is patterned after yours, MLJ. So because I had no other name to give him, he carries yours. I figure what's in a name but what you make of it? So my prayer and teaching for my own family has been to not be that type of person who doesn't stick to his word. Whatever mistakes you make in life own up to them and handle your responsibility. So I hope and pray he can turn that name into greatness by his own merit.

When I was born, you vowed to be there for me when you signed my birth certificate and gave me your name. It seems as though you shouldn't really matter to me since I

The Birth

don't know you as a daughter should. For years, I've been disgusted with myself for holding on so tightly to you. I have not been able to put you in perspective. I have given you far too much power over my life; allowing you to be a great hindrance for me. I've tried to trick my mind into thinking you don't matter, but you do, because I really love you!

After having my son, I had to quit school for a little while to take care of him. That was a very hard decision for me, because some people closest to me already felt like I had messed up my life. Even I had begun to think the same thing. However, no matter what anyone thought about me or my situation, I had to do what was needed in order to take care of my baby. At this point, he had become my number one priority. I had to sacrifice whatever to make sure he was at the top of my mommy list. did not meet my expectations, so I made the crucial decision to drop out of high school for that semester.

I was very determined to return to school the next fall. I was not going to be defeated by being that typical teenage mom that drops out and never returns to finish. Not many people in my daily circle believed in me. I even had one person tell me that all girls say they're going back to school but never do, implying I would be one of them. However, instead of letting people discourage me, I used their doubt in me as strength to go back and walk across that stage. And just as I was determined to finish high school, I was that more determined to be a great mother.

What a long journey it was to return back to high school with a eight month old growing baby boy. After doing homework and seeing to baby who just wouldn't go to sleep, there were many nights I had no sleep at all. I had a lot of class credits to makeup because I was out for half a semester. My senior schedule was a full day, while all my other classmates went home at lunch. There were days when I didn't think I could make it, but when I looked at my baby boy I knew I had to press on. I had a fire burning in me that I'd never felt before. I had to be successful in life even I felt defeated with my family. I worked very hard to meet every requirement for graduation and by the end of the year was graduation ready. What a joy I felt to accomplish one of the greatest obstacles in my life.

As I walked across that stage, feeling proud and accomplished, I waved to my mother holding my son, showing him anything is possible if you try. Daddy, I know that if you had given us a chance to be in your life, even your life would be better. You would be able to enjoy seven grandkids who are

The Birth

smart, healthy, and strong. My high school graduation was one of the pivotal events to which I remember inviting you. Of course, the answer was no. I wanted to share this exciting moment of my life with you—despite all the disappointments I encountered with you. I still needed you to accept me in your heart. I needed you to validate me. Without your validation, I felt useless to myself, to anyone, and especially to God. Yet, I found more strength to continue to forgive you, hoping one day all of my efforts would pay off.

Chapter 17

THE PARTY

One night I went to a house party with my cousin, because I didn't want her to go alone. I never was a party person, which made me feel a little out of place, so I just sat off by myself for a while. Unknowingly, I brought more attention to myself by not mingling with the others. Eventually, this military guy came over to talk to me; who I though he was cute, but no sparks for me. I was just waiting for my cousin so we could leave. The guy continues to talk to me, really helping me to not feel so tense about my surroundings. We began to walk around the house, talking and laughing, just getting to know one another on what I thought was a friendship level. I was not really interested in anything else because I was still seeing the married man. However, I'm enjoying the conversation and feeling just a little more

The Party

relaxed with him. Eventually, we end up in one of the bedrooms because the music was so loud, we thought it would be nice not to have to talk so loud to one another. Of course, that turned out to be the biggest mistake I could have made that night. Once we got in the room, he locks the door and I realize this is not going to turn out good. Within minutes of being in that room alone with him, I had been raped by a guy I didn't even know. As I lay there on that floor, scared that he would cause me more harm and all I could do was pray and ask God to rescue me. How traumatic was that for me. I was hurt physically, didn't know if he had diseases, or if I could end up pregnant again. Once he finished his business, he got up and walked out as though nothing happened. I wanted to just lay there and melt away but I knew I had to get out of this house. I frantically searched for my cousin so we could leave. I never told my cousin what happened or reported it to the police for fear that no one would believe me.

Once I made it home, I showered trying to wash away the horrible act that had been committed against me. But nothing could erase the pain that I felt both physically and emotionally. I could not keep the tears from falling the whole night. I lay on my bed and wished that somebody—anybody—who genuinely cared for me would know I was severely hurting.

I just needed somebody to hold me. I needed to know, was everything really going to be alright?

I did reach out to the one person I felt I could trust to comfort me; the one who promised me that he would be there whenever I needed him. Although he was hundreds of miles away at that time, I felt he would still be there for me. So I began to explain what happened, hoping and wishing he would say something to console me, relieve the pain I felt inside. Instead, I received the cold shoulder, and was told it was my fault that this man had raped me. I was told I should have never gone; what was I thinking about when I went into the room alone with him? I was told I was a dumb little girl and that I deserved what I got for being so stupid.

At that moment, the words spoken to me were more devastating than the rape itself. I thought I would never recover from that night. I could not imagine life getting any better from this point. Little by little, my heart began to grow callous towards men. Over the years I worked hard to not become bitter, but my strength was weakening. My resiliency was fading away. In the following months, all I could do was replay in my mind the bad decisions I'd made. My conscience not only grew a hatred for men, but also for myself. I no longer fought as hard to hold on to love and reasoning for men. As for that married man, ten years passed before I spoke to him again. After that horrible night of rape, I never saw or spoke to that military man again.

My natural affection for men was beginning to change. The seed of homosexuality was growing in me while in high school, and it was starting to lift its ugly head in my life. I thought that maybe it would be better for me to turn to the other side, because men were obviously not my solution. I had no strength to fight to find hope in them anymore. I figured a woman would understand me better and maybe, just maybe, I could find the love and affection I was looking for. Of course, this mindset went against everything I believed, but I figured I couldn't be in a worse place spiritually than where I was. I allowed my heart to feel and accept feelings for women. I never had any particular female person in mind, and had never been in a committed lesbian relationship. I just accepted in my heart that this is where I wanted to be in a future situation. I was careful to keep this thought to myself; I was a preacher's daughter whose mother took a Godly stand against this activity. Plus, I had already shamed her and myself, by having a baby out of wedlock. For the time being, I decided to take some much needed time to heal from a broken heart, and then move on with my secret affection.

I remember one New Year's Eve get-together I was having with some friends. I stopped in the mist of the celebration and secretly prayed to God that he would help me this New Year. I knew the path of life I was on was not the one I intentionally wanted to take. Yet it seemed as though fate was having a field day in my life. In the midst of everything going on, I asked God to guide my life. I wasn't sure if He was already in control, but I understood that I was about to make a drastic move that would affect not only myself, but my innocent baby and those around me. As the New Year clock struck 12:01 a.m., I declared that 1994 was going to be the best year I'd ever had in my entire life. I wasn't certain *how* things were going to change for the good, but I believed in the power of my words.

Chapter 18

REAL LOVE

Thankfully, I never found that woman to love me like I had imagined it would be. Of all the horrible things going on in my life, God would not allow that to be on my record. I realized that no matter how bad the men were, I was still attracted to them. Deep down inside, way deep down, I hoped there was a man on this earth who knew how to love me.

My best friend was telling me about her cousin she wanted me to meet. For several months I fought against meeting him because I was tired of the merry-go-round with men. I was sick of being rejected and mistreated by men, so I decided that I didn't want a relationship. I thought there was no such thing as true love. I wanted to be left alone so I could heal and move on with my life. After my New Year prayer to God,

I was determined to pull myself up and make a better life for myself and my son.

However, my best friend finally succeeded in introducing her cousin to me. He and I talked on the phone frequently over several weeks before I laid eyes on him, and through the course of those weeks, I knew something was very different about him. He began to restore my faith in men again. The desire to crossover to be in relationships with women was fading away. At first, things were happening so quickly, between the guy and myself, that I didn't really recognize that God was working in my life. Remember that New Year's Eve prayer? I eventually recognized God's plan unfolding right before me. God knew that it was time for a change in my life, and that I was absolutely ready for that change. This man was so different from the others that I couldn't believe that this was real. I introduced him to my friends and family, who fell in love with him, just as I was. Honestly, I had never before felt what was springing up in me. It was actually scary to experience, but it was a good difference, one that I needed desperately.

You see, this was one of those moments where God blesses you with the desires of your heart, but then you can't really believe it's happening, so you begin to sabotage it with disbelief. I couldn't believe this goodness was happening to me. The thing is, I didn't necessarily pray for a person, because I gave up on a person. I prayed for a change in me and around me. I began to recognize the positive change in myself with just spending time and talking with him. And with all the talking I'd done previously, no one else heard my soul like this new guy. I was able to really open to up him and bare my every thought, and he never judged me for the things I shared. He was the greatest source of strength I'd ever seen in a man.

I walked into this relationship with plenty of baggage. I had a long list of names and numbers in my 'little black book', which I would pick a person from if I needed comfort that only brought me more disgust. But once I began to see his genuine concern for me....the 'little black book' came of no use to me. Everything in my life began to change for the positive. We started to attend church together and hang around those that would bring us strength. We became committed to one another. That was a huge word for me, because I had never been in a real committed relationship. I had no idea what I was getting myself into, but I recognized it felt right and safe.

I was uncertain and afraid about my decision, but once my mind was made up, I knew I would not make the same mistake my parents had. I was determined to be committed, in good times and bad times. I thought about the impact you had in my life—all the tears and sadness I felt when I thought of you, Daddy. However, when it came to sharing my happiest days—I always thought of you. My king and I decided to get married. Unbelievably, he was willing to take on the task of loving a broken-down young girl. I did not know how to love him or myself, for that matter. Everything I tried to do to show love to previous people proved to be a disaster. But I was willing to learn and try to give what was left of me to my new found love.

We'd only known each other only six months and picked a wedding date for August 6, 1994. Without hesitation, I wanted you to be the one to walk me down the aisle on my wedding day. No, you were not deserving of such an honor, but I saw you as my father, someone I could not shake from my heart. However, in spite of how I felt about you and all the excitement it was to have my king love me truly, you did me the awesome favor of turning me down again. By this time, all hope in you had been diminished. It was like my hope had levels because each time you rejected me, it felt like it was the end. Again, there was nothing left in me to give to you. All of my hope had come to anger. Now all I wanted to do was lash out at you. My mercy and forgiveness for you turned to revenge and hate, again. If it had not been for God, who was there for me, I don't know what I would have done with all those emotions. I was finally blessed to have someone in my life who didn't make me jump through hoops in order to love me. I thought I had nothing left in me to give, but through my husband's unconditional love for me, all the empty places were becoming filled, that I may find the strength to love again. It was as though God wrapped a small piece of Himself in flesh again, to love me back to health.

For many years I was bitter toward fathers and men. I could not see any good in them. I struggled with how to raise a male child with these emotions and not influence my hurt on him. Then I struggled with loving a man, who I can honestly say loves me for real. I was smothering my husband with my baggage. He was doing everything in his power to love me and support me through the night mares. He comforted me through the midnight sweats and cries. He held me through all the hang-ups I had from the sexual abuses. Then one day, I realized that I was taking out all my anger for you and the others who wounded me, on my God-sent. My wonderful husband was getting the brunt of the blow, when he had done nothing wrong. I had to refocus my attacks and anger that I had mostly for you. You had abandoned me; you left me to fight off the sharks when I was just a small sardine. I had to quickly realize I could not pray to God for help, and then when it came, mistreat that help. I had to recognize who my husband was. First that began with recognizing he was not the source to my pain. I had to learn to how to respect him and honor him as he was doing to me. Loving him was not my issue, but being in-love with him became my challenge, because I had never been in-love with anybody. Everything was always a surface love not and in-depth love. I never sought out to love anybody, but only to receive love. My whole motivation for you, Daddy, was for you to love me. That's what I lived for until I got married and then I learned how to love for real.

Chapter 19
THE RELEASE

The countless times I've imagined and daydreamed on how it must feel to be totally free from depression and emotional wounds? I had grown tired of feeling these negative, tormenting thoughts of you. I prayed for many years that God would rid me of this torment. Yes, of course, he did just what I asked of Him, but I would always go back to that emotional slump because I would not accept His purpose for my life. I felt comfortable and justified in my self-pity. These life wounds had begun to take a form on its own, because I refuse to release what I was feeling.

I began to channel that energy into becoming a better mother and wife, but was neglecting to see that my better self was locked away in my mind. I was not focusing on getting myself better, so really I could not be the best mother or wife

I thought I was pursuing. I figured I could make everybody else better while I silently withered away. I was still being orchestrated by my wounds of abandonment and rejection.

Now that I'm older, I understand that you and all my life experiences, have given me the strength to be the woman that I am today. I recognized that I gave more than thirty years of my life to you— years of sadness and depression— many years that you didn't deserve from me or my family. From this moment forward, I will not give you another ounce of my strength. You have had too much power over me, and from this moment on I release myself of any guilt and shame that I thought I caused for how you treated me. I will not be angry and unforgiving towards you anymore. I even release you of any guilt that you may be carrying around through all these years. I no longer need you to apologize or try to make amends to a distorted relationship. I release myself! I release you!

Maybe you have some disappointments or unforgiveness in your heart towards us. But I want you to know—I FORGIVE YOU, I FORGIVE YOU! I even forgive your wife for any part she may have played in keeping you from us. From this day forward, I will be FREE from my past. It has taken me thirty years to lay it all down. I can finally say that I hold no anger or animosity towards you or your wife. I actually long for a relationship with you both, but now, for different reasons than many years ago. Times before, I wanted you and needed you to be a father to me. I thought I needed you in my life to feel whole and complete.

Although, I loved you dearly I could not truly imagine that I would be free from anger and resentment towards you. But now, even now as I write this book, I feel the chains, those ol' rusty chains, falling off of me. I'm no longer bound to the past hurt, sorrow, pain, anguish and abandonment. I had to realize that I'm ready to be happy. I've been rescued by the hook of forgiveness and true love. It is not the fleshly love or conditional love, but by the love of God. That's the type of relationship I want with you. Not the daddy/daughter but by the Ministers of God-type of relationship. However, in spite of all the hardships, God has truly blessed my family to be something awesome. One thing that I preach and believe is that …all things work together for my good to them that love God, to them who are the called according to his purpose, as stated in Romans 8:28. Not having you in my life is, and has been, working for my good no matter how it has made me feel. I have not always been able to swallow that truth, but now I see clearly. No you are not in my life. Nothing has changed between the families. However, the one thing that has changed is ME, which brings me so much joy and peace.

Part Two
DEAR GOD

Chapter 20
WHY ME?

As a daughter, I felt I was unloved and abandoned. I always felt justified in feeling I had every right to be angry. Not once did I consider where my father may have been throughout this whole ordeal. No, there is no excuse for actions of the absent father, however, what I've come to realize is that he is human as I am. I'm sure there are struggles he has had to deal with as well. I'm realizing today that I need to step in his footsteps. What was his life like growing up? As a man, what is he dealing with in his life today? What situations have altered his path of life? There are so many unanswered questions that I now have compassion for him. God, I've been taught in your word that I must forgive. If I want to be forgiven for what I've done wrong, I need to be able to forgive someone else. First Peter 4:8 declares that

....love covers a multitude of sins. Am I calling him a sinner? I am in no way calling him that, but there is fault; nevertheless, I love him regardless of all the years of pain. God, I don't know why you would have me be fatherless, neither do I like it, but I accept your purpose for my life. I don't want all those years of sorrow to be in vain and not use the pain as a testimony. With the many years of searching for a father's love, and coming up empty-handed, I have definitely had my share of hurt and pain.

Now that I'm on the recovered side, I just want to be a blessing to a young woman or young man to let them know they are not alone. I want them to know that they can move on, in spite of the pain. I had to learn to stop playing the victim and be victorious. God, you would not allow me to go through this situation if you thought I couldn't handle it. I had to learn to be the warrior that I am, and fight for my peace, my joy, and most of all my sanity. Rejection is a powerful demon and it will have you searching for love in all the wrong places. Even when you're being loved, rejection will blind you so that you can't receive what God has placed right in front of you. It's only after over twenty-one years of marriage that I'm truly seeing that God gave me someone to help me heal from all the turmoil the past dealt me.

God, I could not comprehend how you could love me, when no earthly man had ever shown me that I was worthy to be loved. Many told me that they loved me, but no one would fight for me. No one could find the strength in themselves to really show me that I was more than just a partner for the bed. I always believed that love was an action word. I just never saw it in action, not from a male point of view. But God you answered my mother's prayer, for someone to come into my life to love me for real, and you sent my king. I didn't know the kind of love I needed. I didn't know how to put it into words to ask you for it. I thought it only came through sex or pleasing others, when in fact that's not what I wanted to do. I had many nights of feeling lonely at the end of the day, because true love was not present—there was only lip service and selfish pleasure.

God for all those who may not have a praying mother, father, or grandparent; I ask that you would allow me to stand in that gap to bridge the brokenness to wholeness. Allow my prayers for the fatherless boys and girls to come to your throne, and I ask that you would receive my prayers on behalf of all those who suffer as I have. We may not all have the same stories, but we may have felt the same feelings or cried the same tears. I ask you Father God that you would dispatch

Angels from Glory to minister to the readers and those connected to the reader that they will be whole in spirit. I command the Angels to stand guard over the innocent and God rebuke the devourer so he can't have control over their lives. In Jesus Name, Amen!

God I know longer ask why me but why not me. I believe in eternity past I told you I would carry this cross. Although this cross has gotten heavy over time you gave me the strength to carry on. Now I see the purpose! Now I'm glad I was a part of your plan.

Chapter 21

THE RESCUE

The power of love can change the course of nature for a wounded soul. That's why it's so important for fathers and mothers to love their children. Sons need their fathers to be there for them, they need their father to show them how to be real men, they need them to show how to love the woman in their lives—mothers, daughters, sisters, girlfriends, wives, etc. The first woman a son will love is his mother, and if the father doesn't think highly enough to respect his mother then what example does that show the son? When there is no proper example, the son's first influence of love is distorted before he can really understand the cycle of love. Just the same, daughters need that power of love from their fathers. Daughters need the father's affirmation to make her whole and feel wanted. A daughter's first love will be her father. If the father is not there, she will likely search in every other area of life for that void to be filled until she finds it. A girl is a receiver, so she will look for ways to receive love, whether through healthy relationships or not.

God gave me what I had been searching for through my husband. When I first met him, I didn't even want him. I'd been through so much with men at this point that by the time my "knight in shining armor" came, I didn't recognize him for who he was. I was not willing to take the risk of being hurt and disappointed again. Many attempts were made to connect us through his cousin, who was also my best friend. I fought my friend for many weeks because I didn't believe true love was out there. I couldn't fathom that God had made a man to show me what real love was like. But God, being the God He is, would not allow me to miss my opportunity on being found. Astonishingly, my "king" was looking for someone to love, someone he could show what it was like to be loved by a real man. He didn't know me or my story, but God did. God had an appointed time for us to meet. Timing was perfect for us both because I had stopped believing in the power of love, and he had just started looking for his "rib" to love. I like to believe God had taken a piece of himself and wrapped it in flesh in the form of my "knight in shining armor" just to show me that

The rescue

I am worthy of love. There was nothing good I was doing to deserve Gods not goodness on me, but because God loved me enough, he didn't hold back my blessing. God wanted me to know that He loved me better than anything I could ever imagine. He knew that I could only receive it in fleshly form, because that's how I was searching for it.

How strange it is, that when we get what we want, we don't know what to do with it. I was so used to not being shown true love, that when I was getting it, I didn't know how to receive it. My connection with love was so warped. It was contingent on how I fantasized it in my mind. I could not express my true feelings of love, because I was so damaged. All these years, I had desired a father's love. What was I going to do with a man who wanted to be my husband? I didn't know how to be a wife. I hadn't been shown how to be a wife. I hadn't been shown how to be in a committed relationship. My perception of a committed, honest, and lasting marriage was confused. So how would I be able to do something that my examples before me were not able to do? Nevertheless, something in me knew that I had to do this. God was giving me the chance to break the curse of fatherless children, divorce, abandonment, rejection, and everything else I experienced growing up. At this moment I had the power to turn it around. In spite of all my fears, God was giving me the strength to tread on new ground. He was allowing me to experience true and new love. I had at my fingertips the best love any woman could ever desire. Was this wonderful man without flaws? Of course not, because he is human too. However, what he possessed was patience, kindness, and integrity to help me battle anything or anybody that came to tear us down. God instilled in my earthly king the wisdom and knowledge to teach me how to fight emotional battles and spiritual battles when no one else was around to see to the break-downs. God conditioned him to rescue me from myself.

Chapter 22

THE BROKEN CYCLE

A child growing up fatherless can be detrimental to the psyche of a child, and affect them as they become adults. History has proven that people who have been hurt, hurt other people. Anger, resentment, hostility, and emotional imbalances often affect those of us that have missed out on that authority figure. Depending on the person it can take a lifetime to get pass was imposed on them by circumstances.

It's time to break the cycle that so many families are experiencing. Fathers are MIA (missing in action) and mothers are out of place trying to hold down both positions. Yes, there are many cases where mothers are not where she need to be as well, which can definitely be just as detrimental. However, there are far more homes with missing fathers. There used to be a saying that babies are having babies. Now these babies have grown up in homes where the young parents were not ready for parenting. And so they have produced a broken generation that is continuing to produce broken offspring. Mothers are way too young and don't understand the importance of being there for their children, and fathers are taken to the streets not being mature enough to hold down their namesakes. Grandparents are raising grandkids because of the reckless behavior of their own children. Sadly the ones suffering the most are the babies.

As a previous young mother, I was lost and didn't know how I was going to take care of this beautiful baby boy. I was neither prepared financially, nor emotionally, to single-handedly raise a male child to be a productive man. Many days, I thought I had let him down because I started out on a path that I had resented and was so severely affected by my whole life, he was a fatherless baby. I had begun to repeat history. The birth father to my son was not in place to be a real father to him. I hated myself for falling into the trap of another broken home. I was a junior in high school, fighting hard just to graduate and make a good life for myself. I was searching for someone to love me and accept me. I was making decisions and not fully seeing the whole picture of what the future may hold for my son and me. I was so full of hurt and pain that I never considered that I might be causing the same pain to my child. I was blinded by my life's tragedies and brokenness. The awesome thing about this life-story is God did not allow it to be long lived. Just in the nick of time He gave me someone so special, which would love me back to health. God gave us both the strength to fight off the hounds of a broken family when He sent me my husband. He sent me someone who loved both my son and I, like we were never harmed by life's circumstances. I began to put on spiritual strength to fight for what God had given me. Only then was I able to go into my prayer chambers and pray against the spirit of single families, divorce, and fatherless children effectively for my family and the generations to come after me.

In spite of the generational curses streaming through our bloodlines, we must break the cycle of broken homes. We need to develop families who will nurture a strong generation of warriors, who will fight for doing what's right. We've got to stand in the face of defeat and tell circumstance that the buck stops here. No longer will I except brokenness. No longer will I except rejection. No longer will I except hurt. It's time to take back the structure that God has for the family. For many generations it has been out of order. Too many hearts are empty and searching to fill the voids that scream "father". The search has resulted in many, young and old, finding acceptance and consolation in drugs, sex, and alcohol.

I had to realize that pain is not who I am. The search to fill the void by all the wrong things was propelled by what I thought. I thought about pain, so I filled my life with painful things. I thrived off of being rejected, so I was rejected. All I thought about was being fatherless, so I embodied being fatherless. My thoughts and feelings literally became life to me.

For many years I resented the word father. I think I could safely say I hated the word father, because of the irrational reactions I would have just by hearing the word. It seemed to be a vicious cycle of self-pity, and I was always playing the victim, blaming all my woes on being fatherless. It was getting redundant and I was wore out from the torment. It was time to break the cycle in me.

Chapter 23

THE TRUST ISSUE

I actually thought that even my God couldn't love me, because He had allowed me and my siblings to experience such hurt. My trust level was in my experiences of all the disappointments. I was so used to pain that's where my dependency to function in life lied. I was confident that God hated me and was punishing me for a sin I had no idea I committed. I firmly believed that 'all men' were horrible creatures and no good could come from them. I developed a thought pattern that my God fit in that category with them. I couldn't help but question what kind of god would allow me to go through this. I was young and definitely didn't understand purpose. I was so delusional and did recognize I had my trust in the wrong place.

Growing up in church, I would hear people referring to God as father. I could never relate to that, because I had nothing in the natural to reflect on. I couldn't differentiate between the Heavenly Father and the earthly father. My only example of a father included abandonment, lack of love, and disappointment. My mother placed us in saint's homes while she went to evangelize, my brother was not very close to us, and my sister passed away from a car accident. It seemed that no one in my family had the same passion as me. Everyone had their own agendas; and I felt that I didn't fit. I seemed to be the only one carrying this burden to be whole. It was as though my pain was going unnoticed.

I even felt like God had abandoned me. No matter how hard I prayed and cried, nothing seemed to get better. I wondered if God even knew I existed. Did He hear me calling Him? Did He see any of these horrible things happening to me? My mother told me He was my father. Was He like my earthly father who knew my pain but yet turned his face and acted as though I didn't exist? I had a misconception of a "father," and putting my trust in God was not one of my considerations. I couldn't grasp how to trust my spiritual father when I struggled so hard with trusting my natural father. Not only did I have trust issues, but I had anger issues with this

The Trust Issue

great big God of mine. There were days when I couldn't separate God, the heavenly Father, from my daddy, the earthly father. Not able to see Him in the flesh, and with my prayers sometimes not answered, I began to feel as though He was far from me and this really stirred up doubt in who He was.

My mother would always encourage me to trust in God. She would encourage me to believe that God could and would supply my every need. I was taught that God was my father and that I could call on Him anytime I needed help. The problem I encountered was I didn't understand that no matter what I prayed God's perfect will was going to be done. Yes, it was my job to pray and to petition Him, but the end result would be what He saw best.

Now here I am, all grown up, striving to be obedient to the call of God in my life. I really didn't want anything like I had experienced growing up. I feared what I would be in Him. I didn't want to be a preacher like I had witnessed in my mother. I didn't want to be a neglectful parent has I seen in my father. I didn't want my new family to be broken like mine had been growing up. I needed to be able to trust in God not only to answer my prayers, but to also heal my broken heart. My heart was so shattered through life's circumstances; I knew it would take God to put it back together.

I was fighting hard against having trust issues with the one and only entity that controls my very being. I once heard a young man say that I am not my thoughts, I am much more than what my hurt tries to dictate. I began to change how I thought of God.

Chapter 24
THE FATHER (GOD)

I began to put all my energy into my new family so that my children would not experience any of the things I had gone through in life. Even when the storms of life came my focus was equally on my marriage to keep it together. Now that I beginning to grow in God, I realized that I had put God in the same box as the human people who had caused me pain. I realized that my growth in Him was hindered by this emotional battle. I began to fight for my breakthrough in this area. Along with this fight I was confronted with the realization that just as it took me years to build up that mistrust; it took me that many more to tear it down. Nevertheless, one of my greatest desires was to overcome disbelief in God. I knew that He could do anything, but the greatest battle had been: Will He do it for me? Will God answer my prayers? Whereas before I could not fathom calling God my father, I can now see and acknowledge that He is, and has always been there for me. He has been a father who was there to dry my every tear, ease the pain, give me strength, chastise me when I'm doing wrong, and to supply my financial needs. The hurt and pain was blocking me from seeing the truth.

Each battle round for healing allowed me to see how far I'd come and how far I had to go. I forced myself to take my power back. For too long I have been controlled by these misfortunes called life. I allowed men to cause me to make bad decisions based on my negative feelings about them and myself. I was continually searching for my earthly father through other men. My demeanor screamed of being needy, not believing in myself, and searching for happiness. Through God's grace, I have jumped some of those hurdles. Not only has my mindset changed, but I see that God allowed these things to happen for a testimony. Even after I blamed Him, and had ill feelings toward my creator, He still showed me mercy to overcome the pain. No, I am not one hundred percent healed, but I am clearer than I've ever been before. There is just a small ounce of residue from the past, but I trust that by the end of my story there will be nothing to detect where my life has been.

The Father (God)

I can see that God didn't hate me. Most of all, I can truly say I trust God, my Father, more and more. Hebrews 1:5 says, "Thou art my Son, this day have I begotten thee? And again, I will be to him a Father, and he shall be to me a Son?" I praise God that He would allow me to be His son (daughter) although I have doubted Him as a Father. Yes, growing up fatherless, and doubting in the sanctity of what a father should be, has caused scars in my heart. I recognize however, that just as deep as those scars are from the pain, I can turn those scars into a mustard seed of faith to trust and believe in the Almighty God. Hebrews 11:6 states, "But without faith it is impossible to please him, for he that cometh to God must believe that he is, and that he is a rewarder of them that diligently seek him." It is my endeavor to equate my faith with the scars that I bear from being fatherless. I want to trust God to take care of me and my family. No matter how difficult things become, I will believe that God will keep us from hurt, harm, and danger. I want to trust God that His purpose in me will be fulfilled.

I thought I could never believe in a father's love; man gave up on me, man disappointed me, and man took away my hope before I even knew how to hope. Now, God is showing me how to turn that shame into glory. Just as little girls are the apple of their daddy's eye, I want to become the apple of my

Heavenly Father's eye, by forgiving and laying down all things that hold me back. And what better way to please him than to believe and trust that he can heal me from all hurt and pain. My purpose and growth in God depends on being able to let go of the past. I never want to forget the past, but I want to use it to build myself and others who have similar hurts. Besides, I'm tired of being beat-up by circumstances I had no control over. For many years, I thought it was my fault that I was fatherless. I wondered if there was something I could have done differently as a child. I carried a needless burden, trying to change something that wasn't my decision to begin with.

As I reflect back over my life, I can see where my Father God watched over me. Being blinded by numerous circumstances, I was unable to see that God had shown me everything I was looking for, in a natural man. At the age of twelve, I was blessed to have received the Holy Ghost. Feeling the spirit of God moving on the inside has been the greatest of any experience. I remember how powerful and fluent my tongues were as I spoke in this unknown language. For over an hour I talked to God telling him of His goodness and mercy. During this time, I believe that I was also telling Him about all the hurt and pain that I had gone through. And just like a natural father would embrace his child to protect and cover them, God embraced

The Father (God)

me from the inside out. He wrapped His loving arms around me to comfort me. He showed his love towards me by giving me the greatest gift of all. His Holy Spirit allowed me to have that one-on-one connection with Him. God was trying to show me that He was my Father of all Fathers. Yes, a natural father was needed, but if I could have just embraced who God truly was to me, maybe things could have been a lot easier for me growing up.

Chapter 25
THE PERFECT LIFE

After the passing of my sister in 1989, I wished that God had taken me instead of her. Not knowing that my purpose had not been fulfilled on this earth yet. There were still many test and trials I had to endure before God's purpose could be revealed. He had to show me he was my only father, not man. I finally had a light bulb moment when I realized that God's anointing in my life is going to come through rejection and pain (no pain, no gain). I began to see that some young lady or some young man was unknowingly depending on my survival through these lonely times. Rejection has such a strong hold on the soul, it can make you feel like you're not worthy of love. It can make you second guess your abilities to move forward in life. It can definitely build up anger, strife and rage. Rejection will make you lose your identity, not only in yourself, but also in God. These have been all my experiences in this situation. I would look in the mirror and not see who I was. I had no father to relate too. Although I had a mother, the lack of a father overrode anything else that was positive in my life. My identity was tied to him. But through the help of God, I have been able to see Christ when I look in the mirror. I'm stronger in the fact that it's okay that my earthly father has not been here. At this point in my life, when I think about all I've been through, tears don't fill my eyes anymore. Pain doesn't live in my heart any longer. I can see restoration in my soul.

For too many years, I have allowed people to stop me from seeing beyond the forest. When I think about my life, I picture little ol' me standing in front of this thick forest of trees, and on the other side is a sunny beach with white sand. It was there all this time, just waiting for me to come through the forest, to bask in the beautiful beach. I have seen this process as being my birthing process into who I am, and not what I've gone through. I no longer want the residue of being fatherless in my life. I want to hold my head up high and proclaim that I am not a victim but a victor. Everything that I've gone through in this life has not been just some bad or good situation, but it has been stepping stones for my making.

As a young child, I asked myself what could have been done differently in my home to help my family stay together. Would I have made better grades in school? Would I have been more aware of the type of guys I attracted? Would I have felt better about myself? Would my self-esteem been higher? These questions come to mind when I think of coming from a broken family. Many fatherless children suffer from psychological and mental disorders. Although there were definitely physiological issues for me, the hand of God spared me the devastating effects that could have taken place in my life, like drugs, alcohol, the street life, etc. for instance, as a teenager, I was once confronted by a pimp who wanted to take me to Atlanta, Georgia—he said I looked sad and he could show me a good time to cheer me up, BUT God would not allow that to happen. The God in me allowed me to know this enticement was a path I didn't want to take. Or the time a young man I went to school with offered me crack cocaine on three different occasions. Again I knew that this persuasion was not the life I wanted for myself. God kept me one more time.

For years, I struggled with issues like depression, anger, low self-esteem, and promiscuity. These were things that mostly could be held inwardly. Often times I refrained from doing things that would make me lose control of myself

The Perfect Life

because I didn't want to add too much more to my pain. However, I didn't realize that I was causing the same damage to my inner-me and my future-me as if I had chosen to do the hard core things. I was having some of the same outcomes. I realized I was addicted to pain and rejection. That's all I thought about and that's all I felt. Although I hated my life and the father that was not there to protect me, I could not find the strength to let the self-pity go.

There was a time I felt so undeserving of good things to happen to me. My esteem was so low and my ego was so fragile. It took me too long to accept the reality that this was the path that my life was taking. I wanted to live in the fantasy that being fatherless was to blame for every bad decision I had made. I wanted to blame my life on all the things I couldn't accept as my reality. I had to understand that my mother and father had a great impact on my life, but I would eventually have the greater impact myself by choosing to turn around every negative experience to a positive one. I came to understand the real facts of my life and it was up to me to decide to make things better for me and my future. Many times my mouth would say what my heart wanted, but my actions didn't always line up with the words. I thought that my life had to be a certain way or I couldn't feel accomplished.

In order to feel successful, I had to beat the odds of just being mediocre. The crazy thing was that I felt like without the college degree, the big house, the nice car, and the smartest kids, I was looked at as my father saw me, as nothing worth loving. While there are some of those things I was never able to personally accomplish, I later realized that my motivation was not from a pure place. I held on to those dreams and desires for my life and if I didn't have them I didn't feel loved. I could not see that I was accomplishing something better, the ultimate task that was raising three potential fathers to love their future families. My marriage and my family were the living proof that it could be done. My husband and I were first breaking an old curse, and then we were setting a new path for the life I had never experienced. Our boys were seeing what loving parents were supposed to look like. Their father was showing them how a man should love their mother. I was showing them how a wife should treat their father. We had set the pace for many generations to come on how to break and keep the spirit of separation from our bloodline. It isn't until now that I see the greater blessing comes later.

After accepting that it was not my fault for the decisions my parents made, and after accepting my fault in allowing their decisions to affect me negatively all these years, I can see that my life's journey has made me the warrior I am today. Many times I felt defeated and didn't want to accept the reality of not allowing myself to heal and move forward. I was unknowingly harboring self- pity for my life's woes. I was very angry and bitter because I blamed life for dealing me this hand. I blamed God for not loving me enough to keep me from the wolves of this life. I thought a perfect life was a life in which there was no pain. I thought a perfect life was full of riches and fortune, no struggle, no hurt, nor loss of life. I've learned, however, a perfect life is to go through all the woes, and still come out on top. A perfect life is to go through the fire and not smell like smoke. A perfect life is to have my heart and lips smiling at the same time, because it's real. I now know a perfect life is the life that God would have me live.

God has kept me through so many things. He's shown me that he has been my father my whole life. Now I can see this so clear. Don't you wait twenty or thirty years before you recognize who you are. I can honestly say my life is not a sad story. Yes, sad things have happened, but I'm on top now. God has blessed me with a few pieces of Him wrapped in the flesh of my husband and our three sons. I had allowed my past to affect my present life, but now I have taken back everything that should have been there years ago. I'm no longer that downhearted, depressed, needy Markeida. I know mountains have been moved from the gates of my mind. I used to feel half-done, but now God has given me wholeness through Him. I feel complete through my Father God.

Part Three
DEAR HUSBAND

Chapter 26
I'M THE FATHER

I wondered what his life would be like. How was I going to provide a better life, the life he deserved? What man would love him as I did? There was no father to cherish him as I did. Tears would roll down my face as I thought about there would be no father of my own or of him to stand by my side to encourage me to push or to tell me I'm doing a great job. There was no father there to experience the joy that both my mother and I would feel in the birthing room.

I gave birth to a 7.5 lbs. 14 oz. baby boy with the one person who stood by my side this entire journey, my queen, my mother. We both laughed and cried together at the site of this little person who had become my reason to live. As baby boy took his first breath into this world, he sneezed instead of crying to let me know he was alive and well. I was so proud to call him my son; at that moment I felt a love that I had never felt before. It was a love that a parent should have for their child. I vowed to him that I would give him the best life possible. I would never leave him, or make him feel abandoned in anyway. I vowed I would show him what a real parent is supposed to be like. I would be his mother and his father as best I could be. He would never know what it feels like to be abandoned by a parent because I would always be there for him. I promised him I would fight for him, no matter the battle, I would be there.

I thought that anything a father could do, I would do. I would teach him how to stand up and use the restroom. I would teach him to throw the ball, how to catch a ball, how to bounce the ball. I wanted to teach him how to treat women. I wanted him to never treat women as I had been treated by men in my life. I would do all the manly activities I could just so there would be no void in his life.

Of course, all of this was a thought in my head because in reality I had no idea how this would pan out in the future. It wasn't until day two of recovery in the hospital that it all really hit me that my baby really had no father. Although I was born with a father, I still somehow repeated history by not being committed to someone who would in return be committed to me—I had begun to repeat a fatherless generation of babies. In the midst of all these emotions, my brother came to visit us and he picked up my son and sat with him in the rocking chair located by my bedside. For the first time my son was held in the arms of a man. The manly strength I could not provide. My brother talked to him and rocked him and held him so long that they both eventually feel asleep together. I realized at that moment, no matter all the dreams of trying to make my son not feel fatherless that I would not be able to accomplish that by being a young, single mother. It may have seemed simple to the naked eye, but I was so grateful that my brother showed up that day to lay a foundation of what a man should feel like.

I took my son home and tried to be the best parent I could possibly be. There were be many ups and downs along the way. There were many days when I needed diapers and formula and had no money. There were days where I stayed up all night trying to calm a crying baby. Sometimes I questioned if I was even a good enough parent to the love of my life. I didn't know how to be a mother much less a father. In the hospital, before coming home alone with my baby boy, I thought I could be all things to him. There were daily challenges and many days I didn't think I could make it to the next day. There were so many struggles I had going on inside of my mind, heart, and soul; and to add to all that by raising a male child. However, I knew I couldn't give up because my baby was depending on me to survive. I had to strive to become a better me, so I could offer my growing son a better life than what I had. My foundation for him was love and attention. That's all I had. I was a broken vessel trying to mold a whole vessel.

Chapter 27
THE WALLS

I just wanted to raise my son to not be like any of the men I had experienced in my life. My focus to do that was altered by my best friend not giving up make me meet her cousin. So after weeks of getting on my nerves about him, I gave in to her. I wanted nothing more than to just talk to him so she would be pleased. Two months after my son turned one year old, she introduced me to this college student. It turns out he seemed to be motivated as I was to advance his life in positive ways. He was reared in church as I was. He was very respectful to me. Even with all the good qualities I could see in him, I still had my guard up to protect me and my son from any intent he had which was not pure.

That first conversation was a bit harsh because both he and I were heartbroken by our previous relationships. However, we managed to have a decent talk by the end of the night. For days, afterwards, we would talk on the phone, chipping away at the walls we built to protect ourselves. As time went on, I became relaxed with talking to him. I found myself opening up to him in ways I had never done before to anybody. I was never the type of person to show anyone my inner feelings but he made it easy to open up to and talk. My days were getting easier to manage. My thought process was becoming clearer. The time came for him to meet the most important person in my life, my baby boy. I was nervous and unsure how this would turn out. I was not interested in having just any type of male figure for my son. I wanted someone who would be dedicated, loving, and supportive. When I brought that college student home to meet my baby, I had no idea he would become his future father.

After knowing him only six months, my love and my instincts knew I had come across the man of my dreams. Within a very short time my son was no longer just my son, but our son. He began to claim this innocent soul as his own. He never referred to my son as his girlfriend's or wife's son but his son. We planned a marriage; something I thought would never take place for me. I had experienced my parents' divorce and a father who had abandoned me so I was not up for that challenge in my adult life. I didn't want to love this man if he was going to walk out the door.

I realized that I was repeating history again. My first repeat was having a child at 18 and the second repeat would be to marry at age 20. My mother married my father when my older brother was about one or two years old. I could see that my mother and I lived parallel lives. So I was definitely concerned that I too would have a failed marriage. My mother encouraged me to not walk in fear. She would say, just because those horrible things happened to her did not mean I would repeat the same outcome. I worried that my son would love my new husband as a father and then he would abandon him as my brother had loved his step-father. So many things, thoughts, fears, concerns captivated my mind. Even in the midst of all these thoughts, I decided to push all my fears to the side, and trust the feelings I had for this man who changed my life forever.

Next came the challenge of living with a man. Since the age of seven years old, I was not used to having a male presence around me, especially someone who had a very strong authoritative voice and demeanor. My mother never remarried while we were growing up. So I have to adjust to this man that I loved, who is also a real male figure. He is very disciplined and orderly, which was a virtue I lacked at the time.

My husband was brought up in a loving two-parent home. My in-laws have been married for more than forty-eight years, and they lived in one location for about forty-five years. My husband grew up with the true meaning of what family should be. No matter the ups and downs, or the test and trials, he was taught by example how family should be. I had never experienced this before. My husband was taught how a real man should be. His father taught he and his brothers how to take a care of a family, how to love and respect his family. He was taught how to be the head of the household (not be a dictator, but a leader). My husband was taught discipline and order, tenderness and regard for others. I was taught these virtues also, but the problem I had was that I was used to it coming from an awesome woman who had to be all those things, when it was equally a man's responsibility also. So, I had to learn to move out of his way. I thought I had to be all these things because I saw my mother be all that to us. I had to recant my thought that I would teach my baby boy everything—I needed a man to teach him. It took me a while to realize that my prayer, my thought, my wishes had become true.

I could see the walls that guarded my heart slowly diminishing. God had given me someone who not only talked the talk, but walked it as well. He was an example of a man and a father, which I'd never witnessed before. I even became a new person by accepting the plan God was performing in my life. It was definitely remarkable to see the difference between my previous life and my life now. We were not perfect, but there was a fight in us to become perfect for one another.

Chapter 28
THE LOVE

Within our first year of marriage we welcomed our second bundle of joy. This experience was totally different from my first child. There was actually a man who was there for all the right reasons. He was there because he loved me and cared for me like no one had ever done before. To have that special someone there to share in the movement of a growing human being in my stomach was remarkable to me. We cried together when we saw the first sonogram. He would hold me when my body would ache, rub my feet when they were swollen; he would feed me when all I wanted to do was eat cold cuts sandwiches and hard, fruity candies. When I was down, and couldn't care for our oldest son, he would take excellent care of him. I would watch as he threw the ball with him, because I was too fat and pregnant to do anything but lay down. Our second baby was coming into a family setting that I had only dreamed about. My sons would be loved by a father who first showed me that I was someone to love. My husband was breaking the curse of fatherless children from my bloodline.

It was time to rush to hospital to deliver our second son. Little man was coming and I was desperately awaiting his arrival. He had grown to full term and it seemed he wouldn't have lasted a day longer. The nurses admitted me in labor and delivery, preparing me for the debut of my new bundle of joy. I couldn't help but thank God to see how He had blessed me to experience this birth with my husband. Through all the pain and pushing, my husband never left my side. He held my hand and offered encouraging words when I grew weary of the process. His facial expression proved he was in as much agony as I was. His love and concern for us eased the pain I was experiencing.

Here we were again, only one year later, expecting our third child. Just as he was there for our second child, he was much more supportive because we now had two growing babies with a third on the way. We went through the birthing process all over again. I still witnessed his tender-loving care for his family. There was a loving man—my husband—there to hold my hand, to encourage me to push when I wanted to give up; he was there to tell me I can do anything. My husband, the father of my children, had become a reality.

I thought for a while that I was in a dream, hoping I never woke up. Then, as time went on I began to fear that I would repeat history. Just as I had done in so many other instances in my life. I started to count the years it took my father and mother to call it quits. Six years to be exact. There were so many struggles I had on the inside. I feared I wouldn't make it in my marriage past those six years. The biggest torment was that my boys would have to grow up without their father. However, by the grace of God, seven years came and went and we were still together. We were not looking to leave the beautiful unit of marriage that God had blessed us with.

Here I had this awesome man that loved me and all my flaws. He loved our sons like I'd never imagined any father could love. Was he a perfect person? No, but his genuine heart and desire to be the best husband and father made him perfect to me. He would talk to his sons with respect and treated them like he wanted them to respond to him. He would chastise them with love like a father should do. He would work really hard for them to make sure they had all what was needed and wanted, and he would make time to play with them.

As the boys grew, I could see them taking after their father. They began to mimic his demeanor and movements. As little men they would wear their father's clothes to look like him. Soon I began to realize that my husband patterned his family from his own upbringing. He was born into a strong stock of family unity, on both his mother's and father's side. His mother's side of the family is like a nation of people. She is one of seven siblings. My husband is one of forty-two grandkids. Every Sunday for many years, his entire family went to his grandparents' home for dinner. They were the real soul food family. There were numerous brothers, sisters, cousins, uncles, and aunts, and they all spent a lot of time together. They always had a shoulder to lean on. My father-in-law is the only brother of four sisters. The family unit is a powerful force. My father-in-law is the glue that keeps them bound together. He was a father figure to his sisters and they all respected and look-up to him for that sound advice and guidance.

My husband grew up knowing the full understanding of family values. He understood what it meant to stick together and to be a person of your word. He strongly believed if you commit to something, stick to it. Because he had that strong background, he purposed in his heart to pass that along to his sons. Whatever he didn't know as a father, he was willing to learn it. He had not only made a vow to love and cherish me as his wife, but to also love and cherish his children. Even in discipline he showed his passion to love them and keep them on the straight and narrow path. He has always been there to fight for them. No matter what the situation was, he was there to show his presence to let those in charge know they were not dealing with a statistical child. He wanted to put to flight any negative vibe anybody would give his sons in the instances they thought there was no support for them.

God equipped him to carry the weight of a growing family and to love us unconditionally. His parents teaching to raise men of valor definitely came through when my husband chose to love me. God showered me with more love than I knew how to handle. I'm grateful for His everlasting mercies.

Chapter 29
THE VALIDATION

Although, I didn't get the father discipline in my life, I did not want to stand in the way of our boys receiving it from their father. I learned early on in our marriage to move out of the way. They needed him to be that soldier, that voice of reasoning. The greatest reward was to see them love him back. When he would get home from work, their faces would light up and their little feet would run to meet him at the door. They would wrestle around with him in hopes of getting the best of him. Of course the three boys were never a match for their daddy's strong arm. They would play pranks on him to try and scare him, but he'd always know there plans and get them first. They marveled at his big utility truck he drove while at work. If we ever drove by one similar they would always think it was Daddy's big truck. When there were parent teacher conferences, I never went alone. Their daddy was always present for the good or the bad news. He has always been there to fight for his boys. He made sure to affirm them through every stage of life.

As we were growing stronger in our commitment to one another, our boys were growing up, developing their personalities, and growing into who they would become. They were now hitting puberty and I was no match for growing boys who were becoming men. My husband and I had become true partners through this process. I handled what I could, and he'd handled the rest—the "boys to men" talks. There were crucial times when they thought, at age fourteen, fifteen, or sixteen, that they were men, and they would flex their muscles, only to find out their dad was the real man of the house. After setting things back in order, he would finish it off with a big hug, confirming his love for them.

I believe that a woman can be there for her children in certain ways just like a father can, but what can be more beautiful than to see a man's man cry with his children, laugh with his children, and spend quality time with his children. Are we perfect parents? Not by a long shot! Our boys have all taken the leap of manhood. They've challenged us to be the parents they needed us to be. We were raising individual

The Validation

nations whom required different attentions. Nevertheless we worked as a team and brought all of our experiences to our family table to create a feast of love, unity, and dedication.

Now, after twenty years of marriage, I sit back and watch each of the boys. I see their father in them; from eating habits, to work habits, to church dedication. God didn't allow me to personally experience this type of love from my daddy. But he gave me a man that had the capacity to sustain a family like ours. We both fought to tread on the head of the serpent to prevent divorce and separation. This blessing will pass on from generation to generation of our bloodline. The men will break the curse of fatherless children.

Part Four
THE CLOSURE

Chapter 30
THE RECONCILIATION

Daddy it's been a few years now since we last talked. I've learned how to truly let go and piece my emotions back together. After nearly thirty years of trying everything in my power to be a part of your life, I finally figured out how to really give all my hurt and pain to God. The only thing I've wanted at this point was to let you know that I wrote a book and that it was about you. I'm still in my habit of trying to protect you, although I never felt your protection. Time has allowed me to know that God was my source for everything I wanted from you. I no longer cry on special holidays like Father's Day or your Birthday or Christmas or Thanksgiving. I've finally become a "big girl" and accepted that maybe this union that I longed for with you will never happen. I mean it had been over thirty years now, so why would I believe that things would change? At this point, I can honestly say I am free and healed from the past.

It's November, 2014, I had a dream about you. Although I'm an avid dreamer, I have never dreamed about you. So this dream kind of shook me up because I dreamed you died. In the dream one of my step-brothers called to ask me if I was attending the funeral and my reply was no because you go to funerals to show your last respects for the deceased. Coincidentally, my feelings in the dream reflected my true thoughts and at this point I felt there was nothing left in me to respect. I wasn't bitter, just tired of the chase both physically and emotionally. After I awoke from the dream, I began to really reflect on it and how I really would feel if I received that phone call. Well, just only a couple of hours later that same day I received a phone call from my step-brother, the one who called me in the dream. Of course, I was afraid to answer that call because I thought this would be my test. Plus, he never actually calls, we normally communicate by text or social media, so to see him calling me was very nerve wrecking. Hesitantly, I answered his call, unsure of what he would say on the other end, I held my breath thinking I was about to receive some devastating news. However, his call was about another family member who was sick and he only wanted to let me to know of their condition. Although I was saddened to hear about the other family member, I was definitely relieved to hear it was not about my dad. My step-brother and I talked for a little while and he said that he thought our dad and I needed to talk. Of course, I agreed but I told him it was not my call on this one—if our dad wanted to talk then it was on him because I had done all that I knew to do to allow him to be in my life. My step-brother agreed to talk to our dad and that was good enough for me. We said goodbye and I did not give the conversation about dad another thought.

December, 2014, I had another dream about dad. Now I'm starting to worry and think the dreams mean something— this is the second dream in less than a month. This time I call my step-brother and I share with him the two dreams I've had. We talk it through and at the end of the conversation he says again that he will talk to our dad. About a week passes by—it is Christmas day and my phone rings, and the phone number and photo that showed up on the screen nearly sends me into a spasm. Instantly, I broke out in a sweat and nervousness, because it was my father who I had not talked to at least five years before now. I didn't know whether to be excited, mad, or what. Because I didn't want to ruin a possibly great moment I held back any emotions that could potentially make him run from me again. At the time of his phone call, I wasn't home, and he had company over his house, so we only talked for nine minutes and seventeen seconds (How could I not time it?). This short conversation felt like eternity because I had never received a phone call on Christmas Day. It was certainly one of the greatest Christmas gifts I could receive. He promised me he would talk to me again very soon. For the next two days I'm almost floating with excitement. My friends and family whom I was visiting were super excited because they know my story and definitely knew my struggle.

It's the Saturday after Christmas, and I decided to give him a call. Not really sure if he would answer, I made sure I was shielded in case he decided not to answer. I did not want to set myself up for emotional failure or disappointment. I had been through enough disappointment and was not ready to open those wounds back up. God had blessed me to be delivered from my past and I refused to let anything come and steal the healing I had received. So I had to give myself the pep talk about "don't worry if he doesn't answer. Just stay strong and whatever is happening with him potentially coming back into my life, simply take it slow and without expectation."

Once I felt better, I dialed the number and on the second ring he answered. I was in total shock and excited to hear him say "Hello". I was nervous and unsure what to say and what not to say. It felt very awkward not knowing where this conversation would go. Surprisingly, he seemed to be ready to talk. We started out very casually, just catching up on family life, and then things began to turn. We began to really talk and dig deep in our past. He allowed me to say and ask things that I'd always wanted and needed to say. But ironically, because God had taken the hurt and the pain away, none of that showed up in a negative way. We were able to express ourselves without interruption of anger and hatred that I had held for so many years. I listened to him and was able to accept him for where he was. I felt no judgment for where he had been in his emotional man. God had recently shown me that a person can only love you out of their own capacity. For instance, if you fill a cup up with water until it reaches the top, then nothing else can fit in, and if you try to force it in the only result is for the water to spill over the realm of the cup. So I had come to the understanding that he loved me to his full capacity. Anything over that erupted in emotional shut down and rejection. I learned that he was in just as much pain as I had experienced. His decision to not be in my life was a result of other factors going on in his life. I understood that and was only ready to build a relationship and no longer rehash the past. I no longer cared to blame him or accuse him of all the things I felt were wrong in my life because he was not there. During this conversation I learned so much about myself, including that I could have forgiven him a long time ago and just maybe God would have allowed us to be reconciled sooner. Maybe I was the hold up in the progress of this relationship. Maybe I needed to move forward and let go of the past. Whatever the case was I could not imagine this conversation being any better. We talked for one hour and thirty-four minutes. The longest talk I'd ever had with my first love, my heart, my dad.

He promised me that this would not be our last talk. He was ready to build a relationship with my brother and myself. He promised that he would be here from this time forward and that he would work really hard to prove to me that he means business. He repeatedly said he wished he had done this sooner to save us all this heartache. I totally agreed with him, however, I recognize that all this bad was meant for my good. All the tears and heartache was a purpose unknown to me, that God would use all for His Glory one day. We ended our conversation on a great note, agreeing that we'll talk to each other very soon.

Chapter 31

THE VISIT

To have conversations via the phone was the highlight of my year. To start on this level was exhilarating for me, because we were catching up on thirty years of separation. One thing I was finally pass was wanting him to jump through hoops to prove his love for me. I encouraged myself to take things slow and easy because we have had a lifetime of brokenness and I couldn't expect things to be fixed overnight. I wanted to build on a firm foundation and not a forced one. Even trying to think rationally, I still couldn't believe this was actually happening—my dad was calling and texting to check on me.

The day I received my first Happy Valentine's Day wish from him was over the top for me. Had I been reunited with my first love—my dad, my hero, my protector, my provider?

Yes, this was really happening. However, although I was excited, I was equally apprehensive about our conversations. I wasn't really sure where he was coming from. I wanted to ask if was he dying, or if he was very sick. I was looking for an explanation for why he began to come around. I could not fully trust what was taking place. I prayed and asked God to only allow his will to be done because I could not live through another heartbreak. My family had gone through enough and I wasn't willing to open myself up for disappointment. I was in a good place emotionally concerning him and I was determined to stay there.

Despite being leery on my part about building a father/daughter relationship, he continued to show he meant the things he was saying. I had never been able to trust his words because there were many broken promises. So when he said he was coming to visit—I totally doubted that he meant it. Why would I believe he would travel to come see me and my brother? Nothing in our past would make us believe this would actually happen. Nevertheless, he proved that his words could be trusted. He came to visit us the weekend of my birthday. What an awesome weekend we had. I could not believe that I had a chance to serve him a dinner plate, or know that he was sleeping in the next bedroom of my home.

The Visit

Those that have grown up with a father may not understand how such a small gesture could mean so much to a fatherless daughter.

We rode around town, taking him on a tour of the city with his seven grandkids who had very little knowledge of him. The one fact they knew was he was not present in our lives. It was so strange having him around that the kids wanted to know what to call him and he replied, "Being a grandfather is a title you earn and I have not earned that place in your hearts." Yet, they were able to call him granddaddy in spite of the previously estranged relationship. Somewhere along the way, many years ago, a tie was broken, but God was beginning to mend the broken pieces.

He was adamant about attending Sunday service with us. Both mine and my brothers' family walked through the church doors with our daddy, father-in-law, and granddaddy. What a spectacular feeling to worship God with our daddy. It was so over-whelming I didn't know how to act. Feelings of joy, peace, anxiety, and serenity filled my mind. We both held hands and did a twostep praise dance to solidify this family reunion. As the service went on, he stood up and had words to express his gratitude for the church taking care of my brother and me. I had never seen my father this emotional over us.

My heart was so full of joy to finally hear his affirmation. To hear him say he is proud of me and he loves me in front of the whole congregation was priceless.

At that moment, for the first time in over thirty years, I did not classify myself as being a fatherless daughter. I was so use to the brokenness; I just did not know how to wrap my mind around being a father's daughter. It was a strange feeling being a daughter to him because I was seven years old the last time I actually felt like I was his daughter. And now here I was, turning forty-one this very day and becoming a daughter to him again. How was I supposed to act or what should I say? I certainly couldn't act like that seven-year-old that I remembered being around him. I definitely didn't want to say anything to make him regret his visit to my home. Yet he was more apt to start those very sensitive conversations. For the first time in my life I could feel his heart being remorseful for all the lost time. Throughout the visit we talked and shared stories of our lives over the past thirty years. This visit was absolutely remarkable.

Chapter 32

THE EPIPHANY

For many years of my life I spent it hoping and wishing for a man to love me. I spent countless nights in tears and thinking hateful thoughts that only affected me. I wanted my daddy to feel the hurt and pain as I had. I struggled with my esteem thinking that if my father didn't affirm me that I was nothing in this life. I could not look in the mirror and see a beautiful person both inside and out. I could only see my past and hurt. I was a reflection of what I felt.

I realized I had wasted the first forty years of my life being stuck in a place that did not benefit me. Of course, there were hurdles I jumped and situations I overcame in that forty-year process. However, what better person could I have been in my teenage and young adult years if I could have only loved myself enough to see that God loved me more than any human could ever do? Not only could I not recognize how much God loved me but I also did not know how to receive proper and healthy love from anyone else. I had this notion that I could only be loved by my father, who didn't know how to love his daughter. In my mind Daddy was the only one who could love me and validate me.

I didn't understand that blocking people out of my life and my heart was the path to feeling lonely and secluded from the true people who were trying to love me with a pure love. There were friends and family who genuinely cared for me and just wanted to see me happy. I didn't know how to let them in my space. For years, I would pull back when I felt I was getting to close to people trying to love me. I had a major distrust for people. I could not entrust my heart to anyone because I always thought they would hurt me like I had been so many times before. Even people I've grown up with all my life feel like strangers to me at times, because of the fear of letting them in my space. The thing I knew how to do was keep smiling to disguise the pain I felt on the inside. My heart and my soul seemed to be screaming for help, but I could not bring myself to open up and let anyone in. What a lonely place.

I'm learning to open more to those I know I can truly trust. God is blessing me with ideas to help others who are trapped in their own minds. What a sweeter life I have now that I come to realize God's purpose. The old saints used to sing a song, "You can't tell it like I can, what the Lord has done for me." Tell your story because nobody can tell it like you.

This book contains just a few of my life's stories. There are many more testimonies God has brought me through. Through my determination to be free I figured out my reason for the tears, now go figure yours out. Get up from that sad, self-pity, depressed place and allow God to give you an epiphany of your story.

Chapter 33
LET IT GO

Never judge a book by its cover, meaning you never know what battle someone else is dealing with on the inside. Life has a funny way of stirring up situations that may be out of our control. However, the one thing we do control is our reaction to the situations. You can allow the downs in life to keep you bound or you can use those same downs and make for a testimony on how you overcame the obstacles. I'm glad I finally came to a point where I could feel whole. Surprisingly, my husband, my children, and even my father could not bring me the closure I needed to move forward in life. I first had to understand that God was in total control. He was orchestrating every move, even the pain and suffering. Then I had to find the strength He'd placed in me to pick myself up and walk out of the despair.

I have never felt as free and clear as I do in this season of my life. I can finally pat myself on the back and be proud of me for pressing through the struggles and becoming a woman-warrior. Are there still some insecurities? Well of course, but the difference is I speak to myself and tell self not today, that's old news and I'm making fresh news. The most important lesson I learned through all of this hardship was to just let it go. Let go of the hurt; let go of the pain; let go of the rejection; let go of the anger; let go of the bitterness; let go of unforgiveness. Let it all go.

I still don't have the finest car, the big house, or the most expensive clothes; however, I'm at a peace I never thought I could feel. No amount of things could substitute for the joy God has blessed me with. My father and I have a relationship that is progressing, which shines sunlight on all the dark places that once overshadowed me. I've always professed my love for him, now it's without borders. Not only has God blessed me and my family through this journey but He has rained on my daddy as well, to live his last days in peace. To God I will forever be grateful.

My truth to you is God is able to deliver you just as he delivered me. Acts 10:34 declares, "He is no respecter of persons." He wants us all to be whole in every aspect of our lives. Many times we blame God for all the things going wrong in our lives. Partly we are right because that's how he gets our attention by allowing circumstances to grow us up in Him. The goal is to not become bitter against Him but to run to Him for strength, peace, and joy. Once you are able to turn to God then you will be able to see that all the hurt and pain you've experienced was only to build you to be a soldier. Don't allow molestation, rape, rejection, abandonment, fear, or hurt to overtake you. I believe you have a greater calling to be free and to look back to pull someone else up from their pit. So you can't stop in this place you are in—this place of depression, anxiety, fear, and loneliness. You have to FIGHT, FIGHT and FIGHT some more until you know that you are totally free from the decisions someone else made that affected you. You have no control over anybody but yourself. Choose today to be free. Take back your power of HAPPINESS, PEACE and JOY. It's time for CLOSURE!